THE BLOOMBERG GUIDE TO
BUSINESS JOURNALISM

The Bloomberg Guide to Business Journalism

Paul Addison
Jennifer Sondag
Cherian Thomas
Carolina Wilson

Columbia Business School
Publishing

Columbia University Press
Publishers Since 1893
New York   Chichester, West Sussex
cup.columbia.edu

Copyright © 2024 Bloomberg L.P.
All rights reserved

Library of Congress Cataloging-in-Publication Data
Names: Addison, Paul, 1952– author.
Title: The Bloomberg guide to business journalism / Paul Addison,
Jennifer Sondag, Cherian Thomas and Carolina Wilson.
Description: New York : Columbia University Press, [2024] | Includes index.
Identifiers: LCCN 2023038839 | ISBN 9780231198325 (hardback) |
ISBN 9780231198356 (trade paperback) | ISBN 9780231552585 (ebook)
Subjects: LCSH: Business writing. | Bloomberg News (Firm) |
Journalism, Commercial.
Classification: LCC HF5718.3 .A32 2024 |
DDC 070.4/4965—dc23/eng/20231213
LC record available at https://lccn.loc.gov/2023038839

Cover design: Josef Reyes

Contents

	Introduction	ix
	Businessworld Map	xiv
1	The Story of Money	1
	Welcome to Businessworld	1
	Joining the Dots	8
	Working with Numbers	11
	Finding Business Stories	12
	Best Practices	13
2	A Stock Is Born	17
	Starting the Company	17
	The IPO	18
	Pricing the IPO	20
	The Stock Exchange	23
	The Stock Index	24
	Why Shares Move	25
3	The Company Story	34
	Selling Bonds	35
	How to Write About Corporate Bonds	41
	Understanding the Spread	43
	Share Split	46
	Mergers and Acquisitions	47

	Buybacks	49
	Dividends	51
	Earnings	53
	How to Write a Typical Earnings Story	57
	Understanding Financial Statements	60
	ESG Data	63
4	**The Country Story**	**66**
	Measuring an Economy	67
	The Central Bank	71
	Purchasing Managers Index	76
	Inflation	77
	Fiscal Policy	83
	Government Bonds	86
	Currencies	88
	Other Economic Indicators	91
	Politics and the Economy	96
5	**The Commodities Story**	**99**
	Reporting on Commodities	100
	The Crops Crisis	102
	The Miners' Strike	104
	Finite Resources	107
6	**Bankers and Investors**	**112**
	Financial Institutions	115
	Financial Products	123
	Borrowing	129
	Financial Regulation	131
7	**Reporting the Story**	**133**
	Interviewing	134
	Anonymous Sources	136
	Social Media and Hoaxes	138
	Thinking Cross-Platform	139

8 Writing the Story — 148
Writing Compelling Business Stories — 149
Headlines — 158
How to Write a Lead — 165
How to Write a Big Picture Paragraph — 172
Quotations — 174
The Rest of the Story — 176

9 Data and Visuals — 179
Numeracy Skills — 180
Using Data Sets — 185
Charts and Graphics — 186

Epilogue: Getting the Job — 193
Appendix 1: Words to Watch — 195
Appendix 2: Bloomberg Terminal Functions for Journalists — 207
Appendix 3: Teaching Guide for One-Day, One-Week and 10-Week Training Courses — 213
Answer Key for "Your Turn" Exercises — 217
Index — 239

Introduction

Business journalism has never been more relevant to our fast-changing world. Every minute of the day, journalists create content about financial, business and economic issues that affect almost every person on the planet. That content is distributed in a plethora of competing formats—the web, newspapers, podcasts, television, radio, social media and mobile apps.

There are more jobs in the field than ever, as well as burgeoning employment opportunities in the multimedia infrastructure that serves the global financial and business community. These range from public relations and investor relations to TV coaches and data-visualization specialists.

The global appetite for business news and analysis is also unprecedented. Financial journalism and multimedia are now mainstream—a far cry from a couple of decades ago when many journalists viewed the business beat as an arcane backwater.

Today, all journalists need to know how to follow the money, no matter their beat. Yet there are few "how-to" books, videos or websites that offer clear advice about the best way to report on business news.

This book evolved from discussions within Bloomberg News's global training team, which has taught thousands of journalists since its inception in 2000 and has helped make Bloomberg News a household name for authoritative business-related multimedia journalism. After 20 years of training some of the world's top financial reporters and editors, the team has distilled its advice into this book, offering guidance to neophytes and experienced professionals alike.

Our goal is to give constructive suggestions to anyone who wants to learn how to write, edit or broadcast or who works behind the scenes in this innovative industry. This book can be used by individuals for independent study or in university classrooms for a semester-long course. We define business journalism broadly because we believe that virtually every story has a financial component. Therefore, all journalists need to know how to interpret the constantly changing cost of money, in all its forms.

A business reporter's main mission is no different from that of any other journalist: It's to break news and get the story right. Yet for every reporter on a quest for the next big scoop, there are countless media professionals in other important roles. They may be creating charts or tables, editing sound bites for TV and radio, producing podcasts or using their news judgment to decide which stories to highlight on a website.

Some are managers, directing the news flow or commissioning new content to play alongside an initial story. Others are "explanatory" journalists, experts in a particular field who have a knack for stepping back from breaking news and explaining the big picture in simple terms to readers, viewers and listeners. In all these jobs, it's essential to know how to build a basic business story out of a handful of confirmed facts.

For decades, journalism students have been taught the 5Ws and the H—the who, what, where, when, why and how. That was the foundation of a good story. It's no longer enough. Journalists need to add two more questions to their repertoire: What does the news mean? Why should people care about it? In the social media era, the **what** of any news is usually known within milliseconds. It's up to the informed journalist to deliver the **why** and the **so what**.

This is only possible when journalists are experts on their beat, when they instantly understand the ramifications of an event and can deliver insights and meaningful context to the end user. By offering some authoritative comments, the audience is better served than when simply being given a litany of facts.

Business journalism didn't start out that way. In its earliest forms, facts and numbers were everything. The town criers of medieval England announced the changing prices of bread, tax increases and the arrival of ships and their cargoes. In the eighteenth century, entrepreneurs and hucksters published prices and information on corn, coal and other commodities in news pamphlets.

As industrialization spread throughout Europe and the United States in the nineteenth century, individuals and media companies started specialized business newspapers and wire agencies around the world. These focused on everything from the performance of stock markets to opportunities for steel, railroad and textile companies. At the same time, business journalism became more critical and objective, eschewing blatant boosterism and investigating the foibles of the financial industry.

More recently, the business media have embraced new beats such as climate change and equality as part of a broader approach to environmental, social and governance (ESG) issues and how they affect investment decisions. They're also reporting more on technology and applying artificial intelligence techniques to produce content more quickly and efficiently. Many business newsrooms have long used automation tools to publish short articles about market moves, but today's generative AI can analyze and create sophisticated content at superhuman speed. At the same time, newsrooms are grappling with the risks posed by AI in an era where disinformation can spread just as fast.

The financial crisis of 2008–2009 and the global coronavirus pandemic that began in 2020 also changed the business media landscape. The financial crisis forced journalists to understand and write about complex financial products such as collateralized debt obligations and equally complex central-bank processes such as quantitative easing in simple prose that non-business experts could understand. Because of Covid, many business journalists became more familiar with health and science and with the use of extremely large data sets to tell stories.

All of these developments notwithstanding, the most compelling business stories still manage to weave facts and figures into a compelling, well-reported narrative. A good starting point is the understanding that any financial data, ultimately, is the sum of human actions—from policy decisions taken by executives and politicians to choices made by investors and consumers.

Like any piece of quality journalism, every good business story needs to encompass a range of perspectives throughout the story-creation process.

That includes not only the reporters and editors who set an idea in motion but also the sources whose views help determine what stories to tell and how to tell them. Diversity in this context is critical.

Business journalism isn't just for people with money and power. It is a way to approach virtually any beat and find stories that affect people across income levels, geographies and ethnicities. The more the journalist can break down the rhetoric and jargon of finance, the more accessible and appealing the story will be.

The initial chapters in this book are designed to explain the basics of writing about companies, markets (including stocks, bonds, currencies and commodities), the economy and finance. We examine these topics through the prism of Businessworld, a six-nation universe designed to enable students and professionals to understand how journalism and business intersect. The book's remaining chapters delve into how to report, publish and broadcast what you've learned and, finally, how to further your career in this exciting field. Now let's get going!

THE BLOOMBERG GUIDE TO BUSINESS JOURNALISM

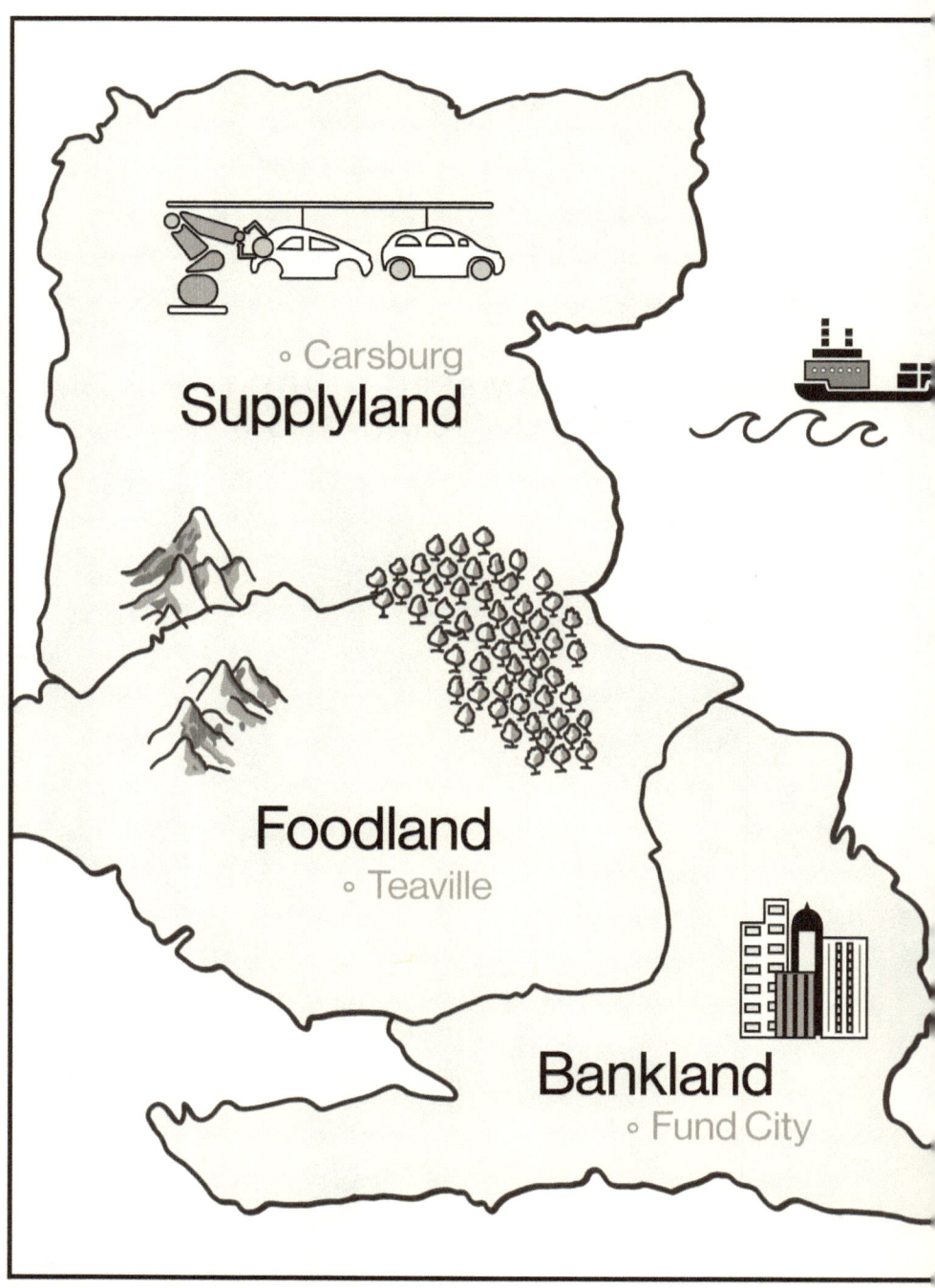

Businessworld has a population of 1 billion people. Its largest economy is Energyland, followed by Commonland and Netland. Supplyland, Bankland and Foodland make up the rest of this world.

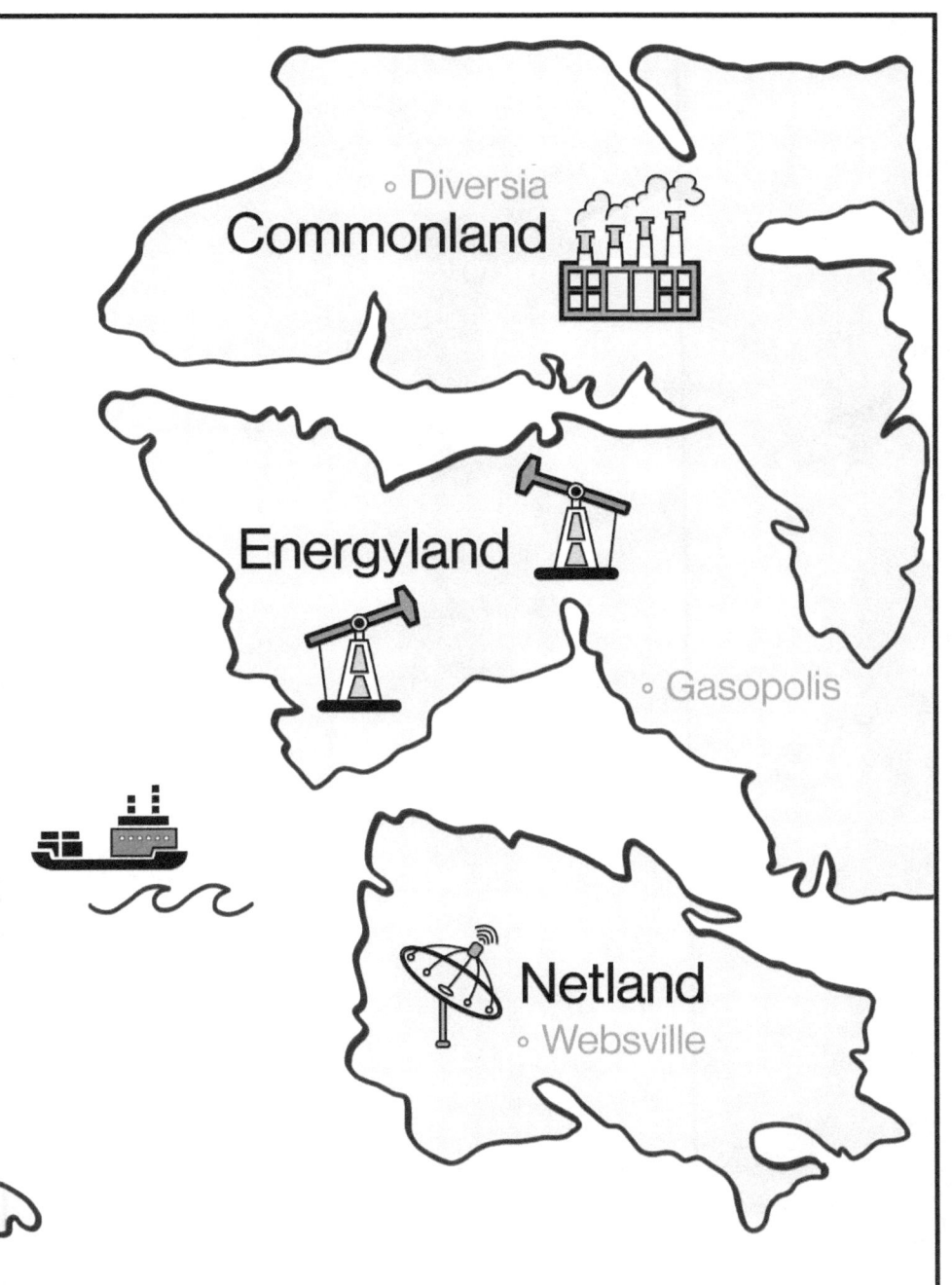

1

The Story of Money

The First Word

"**Follow the money**"—three words popularized by the 1976 movie *All the President's Men*—is more than just a catch phrase. So, too, is the slogan **"(It's) the economy, stupid,"** coined during Bill Clinton's election campaign in 1992. For business journalists, these expressions are a way of life, and this book is designed to show how they think, report and communicate in different formats and on a multitude of platforms.

You will learn the following in this chapter:

- How to use this book
- What makes a business story
- How to combine words and data
- Best practices and ethics

Welcome to Businessworld

The real-life world of business is extremely fast paced. Companies' fortunes rise and fall. Economies expand and contract. Major events such as wars, elections, epidemics and natural disasters frequently upend financial markets, sometimes in a matter of seconds. For these reasons, we created the fictional Businessworld as a way to teach reporting and writing concepts.

You'll get to know the economics of Businessworld through the stories you'll read in each chapter and the exercises you'll complete. Think of the countries as tools to help you understand and report on money and power in today's complex world. By design, there will be many similarities to news events past and present.

The following pages offer a profile of each Businessworld country that you can turn back to for reference.

Country Profiles

Country: Energyland

Energyland is Businessworld's richest economy. The economy is growing slowly. Energy prices are volatile. Automated machinery is replacing many workers. Energyland is trying to diversify into new areas.
The country is the biggest oil exporter.

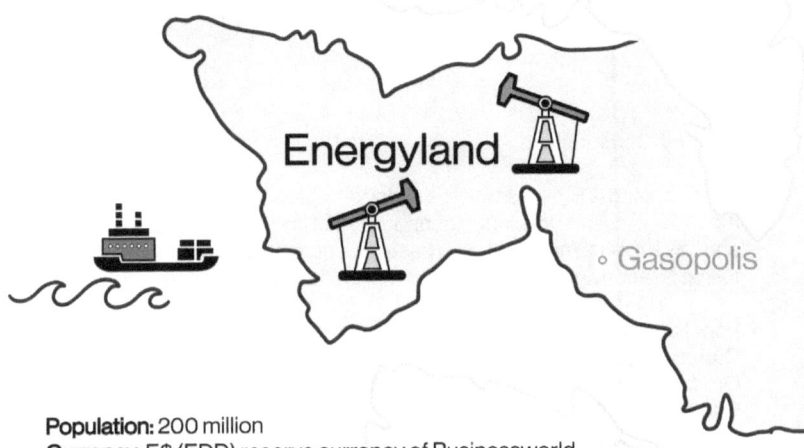

Population: 200 million
Currency: E$ (EDD) reserve currency of Businessworld
Gross domestic product: E$10 trillion
Capital: Gasopolis
Main companies:
- Mining Inc.
- Drilling Co.
- Gem Corp.
- ChemPet Inc.

Main exports: natural resources, petrochemical products
Main imports: clothing, food, machinery

Country Profiles

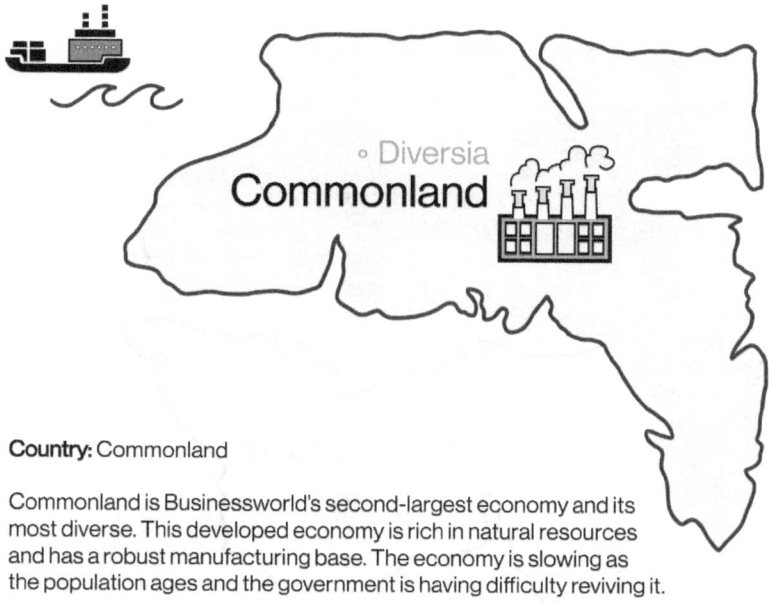

Country: Commonland

Commonland is Businessworld's second-largest economy and its most diverse. This developed economy is rich in natural resources and has a robust manufacturing base. The economy is slowing as the population ages and the government is having difficulty reviving it.

Population: 250 million
Currency: C$ (CDD)
Gross domestic product: C$16 trillion (E$8 trillion)
Capital: Diversia
Main companies:
- GiantSteel Corp.
- Stellarcars Co.
- Commonland Refinery Corp.
- Pureoil Co.
- Commonland Construction Co.
- Hospit Inc.
- Rustic Steel Co.
- Ace Cement Co.
- Prime Builders LLC

Main exports: steel, vehicles, construction materials
Main imports: food, pharmaceuticals, clothing, electronics

Country Profiles

Country: Netland

Netland is the world's third-largest economy. It's growing, helped by demand from citizens of Energyland and Foodland. The jobless rate is at a 15-year low.

Population: 90 million
Capital: Websville
Currency: N$ (NDD)
Gross domestic product: N$9 trillion (E$6 trillion)
Main companies:
    Web Co.
    Driverless Inc.
    Robo Corp.
    Tekniq Inc.
    Imps Inc.

Main exports: technology, including digital apps, social media, product designs, electronics
Main imports: agricultural commodities, processed food, clothes

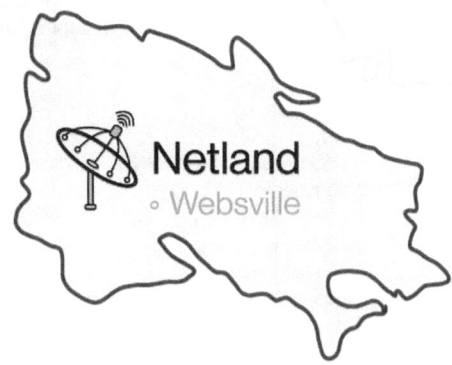

Country Profiles

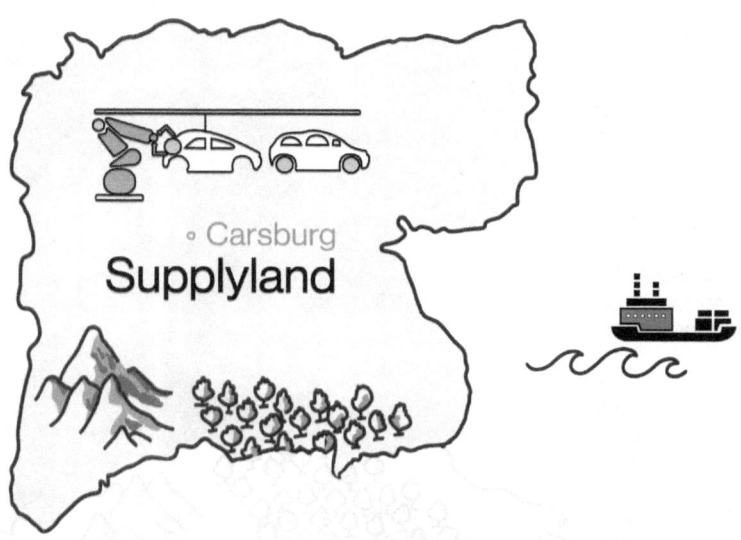

Country: Supplyland

This economy, the fourth largest, is expanding as demand for its electronics, clothing and machinery grows. That's given rise to inflation. Supplyland receives a lot of remittances from abroad.

Population: 150 million
Capital: Carsburg
Currency: S$ (SDD)
Gross domestic product: S$300 trillion (E$5 trillion)
Main companies:
　　Auto Corp.　Keepfit Inc.
　　Wear Inc.　　Phonz Inc.
　　　　　　　　Inject Inc.

Main exports: textiles, cars, electronics, machinery
Main imports: natural resources, food, oil

Carsburg Bondprice Corp. — is the pricing source for bonds.

Country Profiles

Country: Bankland

The world's fifth-largest economy is shrinking. Bank lending is strong but international trading is declining. Bankland neighbors Foodland.

Population: 110 million
Capital: Fund City
Currency: B$ (BDD) is pegged to the Energyland dollar
Gross domestic product: B$4 trillion (E$4 trillion)
Main financial institutions:
    OneBank Co.
    Investing Inc.
    Savings Co.
    ABC Ratings Co.
    InsureCo Inc.
    Build Co.
Main exports: banking and insurance services
Main imports: food, clothing

Country Profiles

Country: Foodland

Foodland, the smallest economy in Businessworld, is expanding. Climate change is affecting crop production and energy is becoming more expensive.

Population: 200 million
Capital: Teaville
Currency: F$ (FDD)
Gross domestic product: F$900 billion (E$300 billion)

Main companies:
Sip Corp. Veggi Co. Peasplus Corp.
Snackable Inc. Flightco Inc. Fizz Co.
Sweeti Inc.

Main exports: processed food, beverages, agricultural commodities
Main imports: machinery, oil, clothing

Joining the Dots

Now that you're familiar with Businessworld's diverse makeup, let's consider what makes a good business story. In the country of Commonland, the population is aging rapidly, and the nation has turned to hiring younger workers from overseas to take jobs in its hospitals, restaurants, factories and stores. That trend recently prompted the Commonland government to make a surprise announcement that it would provide generous payments to families with children in an effort to increase its birthrate.

The news had an instant impact in Commonland and throughout Businessworld, and not just among the happy families. It was immediately clear that many companies would benefit—specifically ones that made diapers, baby food, infant monitors, medical supplies and so on. Stock market traders, trained to recognize the links between the news and the markets, immediately joined the dots. They bought the shares of companies they knew would profit from the government's decision.

Most general-interest journalists don't initially grasp these connections. It's up to business journalists to bridge this disconnect. **They need to know automatically that when A happens, there will often be an immediate impact on B, C and D.** "Immediate," in these days of automated news and automated trading, can mean within a hundredth or a thousandth of a second. That impact could be on a company's share price or the price of its bonds. It could be on a currency such as the Commonland dollar or on a commodity such as oil or cocoa.

YOUR TURN 1.1 Choose two of the following scenarios. For each, write down three or four ways you would follow the money for a news story.

Energyland cuts funding for its free preschool program.

Residents of an apartment building in Netland find out their rent is increasing 30% next month.

Avocado toast with pineapple marmalade is the latest craze in Bankland.

Women working at the biggest factory in Supplyland are making 90 cents for every dollar a man makes.

The capital of Foodland will hold the next Businessworld Olympics.

Almost every story has some kind of business angle. Here's another example that may be less obvious:

Priyanka James is the hottest celebrity in Netland with 25 million followers on Squeaker, one of the biggest social-media platforms in Businessworld. James sends out the following Squeak (figure 1.1) in the middle of an intense feud with Energyland star Michaela Michaels:

FIGURE 1.1 Squeaker sample.

So what happened next? Yes, @Michaela had some choice words for her celebrity archrival, but Wear Inc., Supplyland's largest clothing company, was the one that really suffered. It turned out that Wear gets almost half of its global sales from denim. A savvy intern for one of Wear's biggest investors saw the post and advised her bosses to sell their stock. More investors followed, and soon Wear's stock had fallen 20 percent.

Six months later, the company reported lower sales and announced that its head of marketing was leaving—and that it would cut 2,000 jobs at its biggest denim factory in Supplyland.

Now let's look at the local angle. If you're a business reporter in the town where the Wear factory is based, your readers don't care about celebrity spats or new clothing lines. They need to know what the factory closing means for them and the local economy.

Answering this "So what?" question should be at the heart of every good story. A great business journalist will spell this out in simple language for the reader. Here's where the numbers come in.

Working with Numbers

Many journalists see themselves as "word people" and go to great lengths to avoid any kind of math. But the most talented wordsmiths know how to both analyze the numbers and weave them into the story to make it more compelling. Working with numbers doesn't mean your story needs to look like an Excel spreadsheet. But it does mean you need to understand the math to fully capture what's going on.

Consider these angles from the previous example:

The Wear Inc. factory was one of the highest-paying factories in town at S$15 an hour. Most other factories paid an average of S$12 an hour.

Let's say a Wear factory worker gets a new job at one of these other factories. How much of a pay cut will that worker take, assuming a 40-hour workweek?

$$S\$15 - S\$12 = S\$3$$
$$S\$3 \times 40 = S\$120$$

The worker will earn S$120 less per week, or 20 percent less.

Taking this a step further, let's say 1,000 of Wear's employees go to work at another factory for less money, and 1,000 can't find jobs. What happens to the city's unemployment rate? How are local stores going to be affected? In an economic recession or when people have less money to spend, many will eat out less frequently and buy more food to cook at home. That helps discount grocery stores but hurts restaurant sales.

Now let's zoom out to see how this might play out on the stock market. While Wear struggled, Priyanka James started a new clothing line with Wear's biggest competitor. Suddenly everyone is wearing PJ Pants by Clothing Corp. So if you're an investor who just sold Wear stock, should you buy Clothing Corp.? Let's do the math.

Wear Inc.'s profit margin has fallen to 50 percent. That means for every pair of jeans sold, the company keeps half of the sales as profit. Clothing Corp.'s PJ Pants sell for S$85 and cost S$10 to make. That means the profit is $75, resulting in a profit margin of 88 percent. Clothing Corp. looks like a good investment if PJ Pants stay popular.

Profit margins are just one measure of a company's financial health. (We'll talk more about these measures in chapter 3.) There are probably many angles worth pursuing in this story that go far beyond a celebrity insult. But how do you uncover them?

Finding Business Stories

The best business journalists instinctively understand the economic forces that influence markets, industries and countries.

They know, for example, that financial assets such as stocks, bonds, currencies and commodities usually rise and fall in value on the basis of **supply and demand**. That, in general:

- When demand falls, prices decline.
- When shortages occur, prices rise.
- When there's excess supply, prices fall.
- When demand spikes, prices rise.

They also understand the impact that **government** and **central-bank** policies and actions—from trade legislation to interest-rate cuts—can have on the lives of millions of people.

YOUR TURN 1.2 Write one or two sentence ideas for business stories in each of the following locations:

Your hometown

Your school or workplace

Your country

How could one of these ideas turn into a story with global appeal?

Now choose one of your ideas and make a list of people to interview and possible questions.

Best Practices

Business journalists need to be extra vigilant when it comes to standards and ethics. A simple mistake in a headline can cost an investor millions; an unfair story can lead to complaints from companies and wealthy individuals alike; and trading on inside information can even land you in jail.

Most news organizations have a code of ethics that all its journalists are expected to follow. The most important principles are as follows:

Write accurately, making every effort to verify facts and provide appropriate context. **Correct any errors promptly, transparently and completely.**

Avoid conflicts of interest, whether they're actual or perceived, whether they're political, financial or personal. Don't allow commercial considerations to shade your news judgment because that would undermine your integrity and reputation. Don't pay sources for information or access. Don't accept payments from sources or institutions.

Never break the law or ask another person or group to violate laws on your behalf. Don't be deceptive, duplicitous or dishonest in gathering and reporting news. Be transparent in interactions with sources, readers and viewers. Never hide the fact that you are a journalist.

Write fairly, without bias or agenda. Seek comments from the people and organizations you're reporting on. Give everyone an opportunity to reply to every part of a story that's about them. Ask yourself: "How would I want to be treated if this story were about me or a friend of mine?"

Privacy and Defamation

Following the practices described above can keep you out of a lot of trouble, but sometimes you can still do everything right and be threatened with a lawsuit.

> Bankland's president is known for his cruelty to animals.

> Bankland's president was caught on camera punching a puppy that wouldn't stop barking at him.

In the United States, the First Amendment of the Constitution protects free speech. Some other countries place more importance on a citizen's reputation and honor than on press freedom. That's why it's important to

> Kenji Hargreaves, Eatmore Co.'s chief executive officer, couldn't be reached for his comments.

> Three emails and five calls to Kenji Hargreaves, Eatmore Co.'s chief executive officer, weren't returned.

understand the rules in the jurisdiction where your work is being printed or broadcast. Not every newsroom has a lawyer, but several nonprofit groups provide free legal services to journalists.

Two questions to ask yourself: Does my reporting of private facts about a person serve a **public interest**? Does the public interest outweigh the damage that may be caused by reporting private facts?

Privacy laws mean you can get in trouble for reporting something even if it's true. **Defamation**, on the other hand, is a **false** statement that damages a person's reputation, and it comes in two forms: **libel** (when written) and **slander** (when spoken).

Following the practice of **show, don't tell** helps protect journalists from legal challenges all over the world. Support statements and assertions with facts, figures, anecdotes and examples. Avoid adjectives, hyperbole, characterizations and labels that may show bias and cause the reader to question the story's credibility.

YOUR TURN 1.3

It's possible to defame someone during the course of your reporting. Be careful how you frame questions and what you write in emails. Make a list of any problems you see with the following email, which a reporter wrote to a source who is on the board at Sweeti Inc. Explain why they are problems.

Hey Kiana,

Thanks for the tip about last week's board meeting. I owe you a fancy dinner — with champagne, of course! I need your help on something else. I'm hearing that your chief financial officer is in deep trouble. One of my sources, who works in Sweeti's accounts division, told me off the record that she was instructed to inflate second-quarter sales figures.

I'm planning to report this tomorrow — so please let me know!
Then we can really celebrate!

Yours truly,
Ace Reporter

The Final Word

After reading this chapter, you should have a basic understanding of what makes a business story, why it's important to "follow the money" and the ethical principles around gathering financial news. The next chapter will teach you how markets actually work.

2

A Stock Is Born

The First Word

Financial markets never sleep. In an age of 24-7 electronic trading, trillions of dollars of financial assets—stocks, bonds, currencies and commodities—change hands every day around the world.

The next few chapters of this book will dive into markets and show you how to report on them. In this one, **we will focus on stocks, also known as shares, securities or equities.** Companies sell stock to raise money. Individuals and institutions buy those shares as investments and in the hope their price will rise. When you buy stock, you own part of a company.

You will learn the following in this chapter:

- Why companies sell shares
- How shares are sold: the initial public offering (IPO) process
- How to report on IPOs and the stock market
- Why shares move: earnings, market speculation, valuation

Starting the Company

To understand stocks, it helps to look at how a simple idea turns into a company owned by individual investors. Let's take the example of the start-up Sip Corp. It all began when Jameel Smith and Lisa Ogawa met at Foodland Business School and decided to start an energy-drinks company. After graduation, they formed Sip Corp. with money pooled from their savings. The initial capital enabled them to lease an office, hire a few workers, rent a small factory and set up a retail network.

Sip quickly became a success. There was so much customer demand for the drinks that they couldn't produce enough at their factory. So Smith, now the chief executive officer, and Ogawa, the chief financial officer, decided it would be a good time to invest in a second factory.

They estimated that this would cost about F$15 million. But they didn't have that kind of money. They had a few options for raising funds:

A. Borrow money from a bank
B. Sell bonds to raise money
C. Sell part of their stake in Sip via an initial public offering, or IPO

Smith and Ogawa went with option C after agreeing that borrowing from a bank or selling bonds would mean getting into debt. By selling shares, they could remain essentially debt-free while generating capital to expand and increasing public awareness of the company. The downside of "going public" is that the company would have to comply with more regulations and be accountable to shareholders. (See more about bonds versus stocks in chapter 3.)

The IPO

Smith and Ogawa owned 100 percent of Sip when they formed the company and issued themselves 2.5 million shares. They met with bankers and decided to sell 20 percent of their holding, or 500,000 shares, via an initial public offering to raise the F$15 million for a second factory. After the IPO, their stake in Sip dropped to 80 percent.

What's an IPO?

When shares are sold to the public for the first time, it's called an initial public offering, or an IPO.

The shares are sold in what's called the primary market. The money raised from the sale of shares goes to the company. Investors who buy the shares become shareholders or co-owners of the company.

Investors buy the shares for two main reasons. First, they hope to receive a share of the company's profits by way of dividends. For example, the company may announce an annual dividend of F$10 for every share an investor holds. However, the company isn't obliged to give shareholders a dividend.

Second, they hope that the company's share price will rise when the shares are listed on the stock market. This is where trading between investors happens. As such, this is known as the secondary market.

Note that shares and equities mean the same thing.

Smith and Ogawa, who were the issuers of the IPO, appointed Foodland Bank as the **lead manager** for the share sale. Foodland Bank then appointed other banks and formed what's known as a **syndicate** to help manage the sale.

The syndicate's role was to help Sip market the IPO to potential investors and to enable regulatory approvals. The syndicate also **underwrites** the IPO. This means if investors don't buy all the shares on offer, the underwriters promise to buy the unsold ones and try to sell them.

Foodland Bank said it would be the **lead underwriter**, or **bookrunner**, meaning it would sell the largest proportion of the shares in the IPO. Sip paid a fee to the banks in return for their services, with the largest amount going to Foodland Bank.

The banks started work on the initial public offering. Foodland Bank filed a **preliminary prospectus**, also sometimes known as a **red herring** prospectus, with Foodland's stock market regulator. In this document, the bank provided details such as the purpose of the share issue, Sip's financial reports, a description of its management team and so on.

Two weeks later, the regulator approved the draft plan after seeking some clarifications. Foodland Bank then filed a prospectus that included information from the draft and an explanation of how Sip planned to price its shares. Foodland's regulator approved the share sale (figure 2.1).

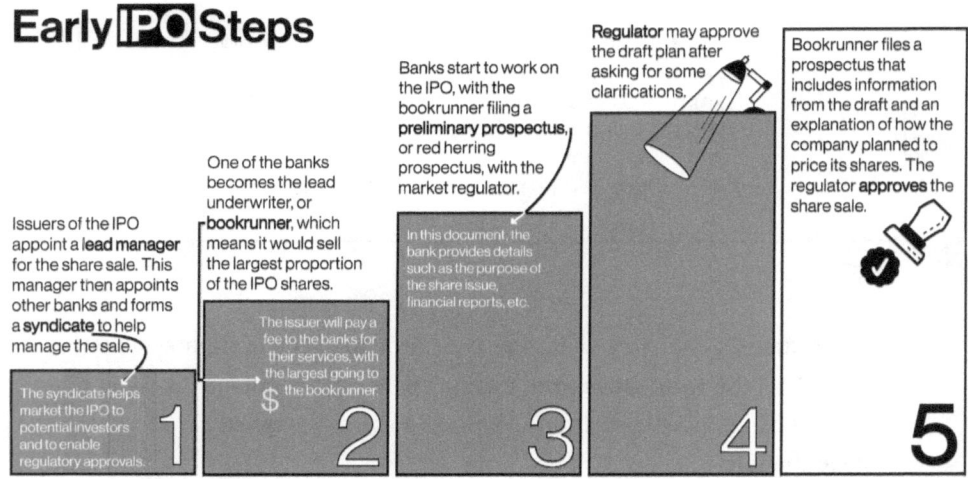

FIGURE 2.1 Early IPO steps.

Pricing the IPO

Foodland Bank's next challenge was to determine the price at which Sip's shares could be offered to the public. The lead managers led by Foodland

Bank announced Sip's IPO plans in advertisements in the *Foodland Times* and on social media.

They invited investors to bid for shares within a **price band** determined by the lead managers during a one-week period. In this case, the

Finding the news in an IPO announcement:
How much money does the company plan to raise? Why is the company going public? How many shares are being sold? What's the IPO price band? When will the offer start, and close? What percentage of the company's capital does the IPO represent? What's the value of the IPO at the top end of the price band? Who are the lead managers?

Reporting on investor response to the IPO:
At what price did the company offer shares to anchor investors? Did the company sell the shares at the top, lower or mid-end of the price range? What does that show about demand for the offer? Who are the anchor investors? How many shares will the company sell to them? How much money will the company raise from them?

Reporting before trading begins:
Was the IPO oversubscribed or undersubscribed? Why? What is the value of the IPO at the top end of its price band? What number of shares were reserved for employees? What amount was raised from anchor investors? By how much did the owners reduce their stake in the company?

Reporting on the listing day:
Are the shares trading above or below the IPO price? Why? How have the shares performed? Did they rise or fall? Did the underwriters exercise an option to sell additional shares, commonly known as a greenshoe or over-allotment option?

PRO TIP

A good reporter doesn't wait for a press release to write the above stories. She builds sources within investment banks, brokerages and companies to be the first to break news throughout the IPO process. That might include writing stories on the company's plans to raise money and why, or about the reasons for investors' appetite for an IPO.

band was F$30 to F$40 per share, and investors had to state the price at which they were willing to buy the shares. This is the norm in what's called a **book-building process**.

One day before the IPO opened for public bidding, the IPO managers offered the shares to **anchor investors**. These are usually big brokerage houses and investment banks. Offering shares to anchor investors is a requirement by several stock market regulators around the world because it helps the public gauge how much demand there is from what are known as **institutional investors** and the price that they're willing to pay. It helps companies, too, because it ensures a certain portion of the IPO is sold.

Once smaller investors have had their turn bidding, the lead managers select the most popular price—the price with the largest number of bids. If the number of shares that have been bid for exceeds the number of shares on offer, which is often the case, the shares are distributed by drawing lots. The total number of shares after the IPO is often referred to as the company's **shares outstanding**.

YOUR TURN Write a headline and three paragraphs about Sip's IPO plans based on what you've learned so far.

2.1

The Stock Exchange

After the lead managers allocated Sip's shares to investors, they helped Sip "list" its shares on the Foodland Stock Exchange at a splashy event.

Sip was able to sell 500,000 shares in the IPO priced at F$35 each, the middle of its advertised range. That meant the company raised F$17.5 million (F$35 a share × 500,000 shares) in the IPO, more than enough to cover its second factory and pay fees to the banks.

But remember, Sip only sold 20 percent of the company. The other 80 percent, still owned by Smith and Ogawa, was now valued at F$70 million (F$35 a share × 2 million shares) on the basis of the amount raised, giving the company a total value of F$87.5 million (20 percent stake sold to the public + the original owners' stake).

That value rose after trading began on the exchange. Sip's shares jumped 16 percent to F$40.60 as soon as the market opened and ended the day 13 percent higher at F$39.55. In other words, some investors considered the company to be more valuable than its IPO price.

PRO TIP

Focus on **why** a stock is up or down. How a company's value moves can signal to the reporter that there's a bigger story to tell about the company, the industry or even the state of the economy. When shares surge, find out why investors are lapping them up. And vice versa. Follow the money!

Sip's price rises or falls depending on the **demand** for and the **supply** of the shares. Investors **bid** to buy them at a particular price and quantity. Sellers **offer** their shares in the same way. When the buyers and sellers agree on a price, usually via a trading platform, the shares change hands.

YOUR TURN 2.2 — You're a TV reporter on the floor of the Foodland Stock Exchange. How would you report on Sip's first day of trading? Come up with a script of no more than 150 words.

The Stock Index

Generally, when people talk about how a stock market is performing, they are referring to the shares of companies that trade on a particular index.

Sip, Veggi Co. and Snackable Inc. are three of the 500 or so companies that trade on the Foodland Stock Exchange, for instance.

So how does one keep tabs on how Foodland's stock market is doing?

Foodland, like other countries, has a benchmark stock index comprising the largest stocks by market capitalization. Foodland's index is called the Fex Index, and it's the **benchmark index** of the country in the same way that the S&P 500 Index and the Dow Jones Industrial Average are the benchmark indexes of the United States.

Foodland also has a separate index for food companies, called the Foodstock Index. Sip, Veggi and Snackable are among the 20 companies on this index.

What is market capitalization?

Market capitalization is the price of a company's share multiplied by the total number of outstanding shares. The market cap, or market value, shows how valuable a company is over time and compared with other companies.

Stock market journalists strive to tell their readers and viewers what stocks and industries are rising or falling on a particular index, and, most important, **why**. For example, why are investors buying shares of Sip? Why are they selling shares of Veggi and Snackable? Why are technology stocks rising more than those of food companies? Why now?

A good reporter also explains the **broader significance** of the stock market's price changes. Is today's decline a blip or has it been going on for several days? Is today's gain the biggest since a particular date? Are there political or economic reasons behind the market's changes, such as the likelihood of an election, trade tensions with other countries or the possibility of a recession?

YOUR TURN 2.3 Answer the following questions.

1. Sip has a million shares outstanding. Its shares closed today at F$32. What is the company's market capitalization?

2. Veggi today reported net income for the year of F$1.5 million on sales of F$14.25 million. Its shares closed at F$25.70 per share. Veggi has 1.2 million shares outstanding. What is the company's market value?

3. Snackable's shares have tripled this year to F$30 a share. The company has 5.2 million shares outstanding. How much has the company's market value gained since Jan. 1?

Why Shares Move

There are countless reasons why companies' shares rise or fall. These include management changes, merger and acquisition activity, weather-related events, supply-demand disruptions and changes in recommendations by analysts.

News from competitors and broader market optimism or pessimism could also affect demand for a company's stock.

Here are additional four scenarios that can move shares higher or lower:

- When a company announces its earnings (revenue, profit, dividend, etc.)
- When there's market speculation about a forthcoming company event
- When a company's valuations are considered excessive or surprising
- When technical indicators suggest shares have been overbought or oversold

Let's take a brief look at each of these scenarios for Sip.

EARNINGS

At 9 a.m. on Oct. 15, Sip Corp. posted the company's profit, or earnings, for the third quarter of the year, from July 1 to Sept. 30. Sip's **net income** had risen 52 percent to a record F$3.3 million compared with the figures in the same period a year earlier. Net income is the most frequently reported form of profitability and is often known as **the bottom line**. Another important metric that shows profitability is **earnings per share**, or **EPS**, which is net income divided by the number of outstanding shares.

Sip also said the sales outlook, or **forecast**, for the fourth quarter was better than it had previously expected. (See chapter 3 for more on profit and forecast.)

Within 30 minutes of the announcement, Sip's shares had risen 8.3 percent. That was the biggest increase since the 9 percent jump when the stock started trading about 5 months earlier.

The *Foodland Times* website published the headline below, and its affiliated TV station, FTV, ran it as a banner headline during the morning news program:

Sip Surges Most in Five Months After Record Profit
Sip is the biggest-weighted stock on the Fex Index.
   On the day of Sip's earnings, the index rose 3.6 percent, the most in 15 months.

The percentage change in a stock or an index often doesn't tell the full story. It's necessary to compare that change with the historic performance of the stock or the index. Check whether the move was the biggest percentage increase since a particular date or whether it was at its highest (or lowest) level since a certain date.

Look for relative value and find superlatives like the highest, lowest, biggest rise/drop, first time in three months and so on to help explain the number. That will help answer "what" the stock/index did.

Also, a good stocks story always has a "why" in the headline and lead so that readers immediately know the cause of the rise or decline.

The why is usually a "fundamental" or known reason, such as an increase in company profit or an analyst downgrading a stock. It could be a company replacing its chief executive officer or buying another company.

The contribution of a stock to the performance of an index depends upon the stock's weight on the index. The weight of a stock is the market capitalization of the stock divided by the total market value of all the shares in an index.

For example, if one company's market value is $8 million and the cumulative value of all the stocks in an index is $50 million, that company's weight is 16%.

The *Foodland Times* stock story read as follows:

Foodland Stocks Jump Most in 15 Months on Record Sip Earnings
Foodland stocks surged the most in 15 months, led by Sip Corp., after the energy-drinks maker reported record profit and said the sales outlook for the rest of the year was better than previously forecast.

The Fex Index gained 3.6 percent at the close of trading on the Foodland Stock Exchange. Sip rose 8.3 percent after it posted third-quarter net income of F$3.3 million, helped by the introduction of its new Cherry Energy drink line.

MARKET SPECULATION

On another occasion, years later, Sip's shares dropped 5.7 percent to F$22, the lowest level in seven months.

The reporter at the *Foodland Times* called the company and inquired about the decline. Sip said it had no comment.

The reporter called Ron Bison, a trader at Foodie Brokerage Inc. Bison tracks the company's performance and has a "hold" recommendation on the stock. This means he suggests that investors neither add to nor sell their Sip shares. Bison said there was speculation in the market that Sip was planning to buy Veggi.

Such a large purchase could be seen as risky for Sip investors and positive for Veggi investors. That's because Sip would probably have to offer a higher price than Veggi shares currently trade at to complete the deal. Sip and Veggi both told the reporter that they did not comment on speculation.

The reporter wrote this story:

Sip Plunges to Seven-Month Low on Speculation About Veggi Purchase

Sip Corp. declined to a seven-month low on speculation the energy drinks maker plans to buy Veggi Co.

Sip shares dropped 5.7 percent while Veggi rose 2.4 percent. Sip and Veggi declined to comment on the speculation.

"The purchase could be bad news for Sip because Veggi has a lot of debt," said Ron Bison, a trader at Foodie Brokerage Inc. Bison has a hold recommendation on the stock, which closed today at F$22 a share. His 12-month price target for Sip is F$30. "For Sip, the risks outweigh the gains in this transaction."

give me the **INTEL**

Stocks sometimes rise or fall because of "speculation" in the market. A rumor per se is not news. But when a rumor moves the price of a stock, it becomes speculation and may be worth reporting. A quote from a reputable trader or an investor saying that the stock is moving because of the speculation is essential.

VALUATION

A few months later, Sip's shares advanced 12.2 percent in a week. That was a record weekly advance.

The *Foodland Times* reporter called Sip to check why the shares were rising. A company spokesperson said she didn't know of any specific reason.

The reporter called Ron Bison, the trader at Foodie Brokerage. He said the stock had been rising because a key performance indicator—in this case, the **estimated price/earnings ratio**, also known as the forward P/E ratio—showed that the stock was inexpensive relative to the company's anticipated profits. (See chapter 3 for more on key performance indicators.)

REPORTER: "What do you mean by that, Ron?"
BISON: "Well, when I compare the price of Sip shares with its estimated profit over the next four quarters, they seem to be pretty cheap. So traders and investors are trying to take advantage of this by buying the shares."
REPORTER: "So they're cheap relative to what?"
BISON: "In this case, Sip's P/E is 9, which is the lowest in three years. But Sip's also cheap compared with its competitors."

The reporter's story:

Sip Has Record Weekly Gain as Stock Seen Cheapest in Three Years
Sip Corp. had a record weekly gain as recent declines in the stock made it the cheapest in three years relative to earnings.

The stock is trading at nine times its estimated 12-month earnings, which is the lowest in three years, according to Ron Bison, a trader at Foodie Brokerage Inc.

Stocks rise or fall when analysts and investors consider them either undervalued (cheap) or overvalued (expensive).

The price/earnings ratio is one common metric by which stocks are valued.

The higher the P/E ratio compared with its historical levels or versus its peers, the more expensive the stock is relative to its earnings and vice versa.

Price/Earnings = Current stock price divided by the earnings per share (EPS) of the past 12 months. The result is a multiple. For example, if the stock is trading at $36 and the earnings per share is $4, the multiple is 9. This means investors are willing to pay $9 for every $1 of earnings.

Estimated Price/Earnings = Current stock price divided by the estimated earnings per share for the next 12 months. For example, if the current price is $30 and the estimated EPS is $2 per share, the estimated P/E ratio for the next one year is 15.

How do we determine that a stock is expensive or cheap by looking at the P/E multiple? Compare the ratio to the company's historical levels or against its peers to determine that. P/E on its own doesn't mean anything.

If the multiple 9 is the highest in five years, you could say that the stock is the most expensive in five years relative to its earnings. Or that the stock is trading at 9 times its trailing 12-month earnings.

Note, a higher P/E could also mean investors expect a faster rate of growth for the company.

TECHNICAL ANALYSIS

Near the end of the year, Sip's shares fell 14 percent in a week.

A *Foodland Times* editor asked the reporter to write a story about the stock's decline and the outlook for the following year. The reporter called analysts and investors, but they didn't know of any fundamental reason for the stock's drop. So the reporter decided to speak with technical analysts.

How do technical analysts differ from fundamental analysts?

Fundamentals analysts make predictions about a stock's outlook based on fundamental factors such as the state of the economy, a change in senior management, speculation about a purchase or sale and other supply-and-demand considerations. They focus on why a stock or an index could rise or fall.

Technical analysts only look at the price of a security — a stock, bond, commodity or currency. They believe that by looking at patterns of price movements, they can determine when investor demand is going to change direction. If the price of a stock moved in a particular way in the past, that trend will recur, according to the technical analysts.

Some traders examine different technical indicators to estimate the future price of a security.

One commonly used indicator is called the relative strength index, known as the RSI. Technical investors view the RSI to track whether a security has risen or fallen too much — in other words, has it been overbought or oversold — and hence whether it's poised to move in the opposite direction.

The reporter wrote the following story using a chart and some text:

Sip May Rebound as Technical Gauge Shows Stock Cheapest in a Year

Sip Corp. may rebound after a technical indicator suggested that the energy-drink maker's shares have tumbled too far, too fast.

The stock's relative strength index declined below 20 for the first time in a year. When an equity's RSI drops below 30, technical analysts generally consider it to be oversold and say that the stock is poised to rebound.

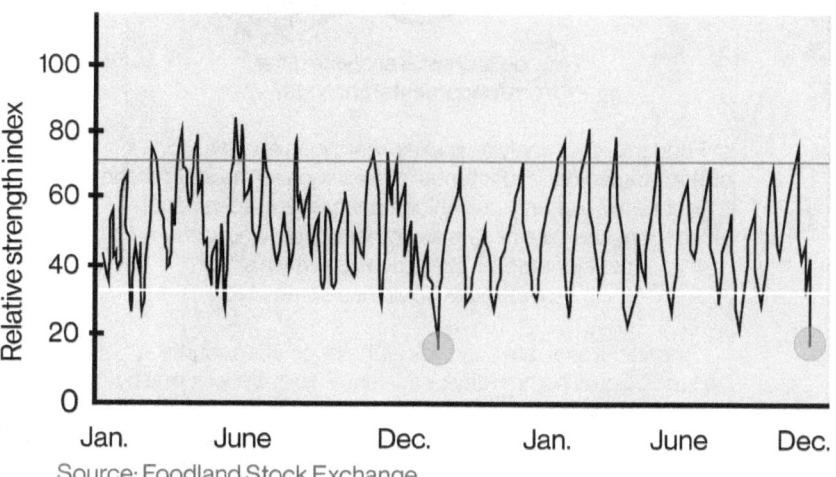

FIGURE 2.2 **Debt woes.**

YOUR TURN 2.4 — It's Oct. 20. Use the details below to write a four-paragraph story about the performance of Foodland's stock market today.

Fex Index closed 3.8% higher at 1516.35, a record.

Peasplus Corp., which grows and sells vegetables, announced better-than-expected third-quarter earnings and said the sales outlook for next year was "very strong." The stock jumped 4.6% to a record F$26.

Peasplus is Foodland's bellwether stock because it is routinely the first major company to report the previous quarter's earnings. Therefore, it gives investors their first peek into Foodland's corporate performance.

Foodland's main industry is agriculture. Foodland had a bumper harvest this year because of favorable weather.

Peasplus and other food stocks pushed the Fex Index higher.

Analysts were surprised by Peasplus's earnings. Several brokerages including Cheese Analysis Inc. and Butter Analytics Co. plan to raise their earnings estimates for Foodland companies.

Michelle Chua, managing director and market strategist at Teaville-based Toe Stock Broking Co., said: "There's a lot of foodgrain out there at present. The problem is that with the low prices, farmers have been reluctant to sell, so there's a lot of on-farm storage and farmers have foodgrains tucked away."

"Peasplus's earnings were stunning. They're a harbinger of good times for all companies in Foodland. We will look at our estimates for other companies again, which at the moment seem very conservative."

The Final Word

Stock market reporting is a vital and vigorous job, demanding unrelenting curiosity, a sense of urgency and the ability to switch gears in an instant.

Typically, stock market journalists follow both fundamental and technical movements. They strive to tell their audiences why price changes are significant and how they affect the company, its competitors, the stock market and the broader economy.

3

The Company Story

The First Word

After the fanfare of an initial public offering (IPO), a public company faces far more obligations than it did as a private one. Put simply, it's now accountable to its public shareholders. That means it needs to report earnings quarterly or semiannually and inform regulators about any major changes to its business, such as selling debt (or more stock) or buying another company.

Collectively, these events are known as **corporate actions**, and they are staples of company coverage. The journalist helps investors understand the news by looking beyond routine press releases. An earnings report that looks positive on the surface may mask deeper problems. A "friendly" acquisition plan could turn hostile. A new product launch may conceal years of disappointment and frustration.

It takes **exceptional news judgment**, **flexibility, persistence, skepticism** and **deep sourcing** to break the kind of company stories that have lasting impact and attract millions of readers, listeners and viewers around the world.

This chapter tracks some of the main events in the life of **Sip Corp.**, the energy-drinks maker based in Foodland. It also addresses some of the environmental, social and governance issues that are increasingly part of the company story.

THE COMPANY STORY • 35

You will learn the following in this chapter:

- How a company raises funds by selling bonds
- How to understand bond coupons and yields
- How to write stories about corporate bonds
- How to understand and write about stock splits, mergers and acquisitions, buybacks and dividends
- The basics of earnings coverage
- How to understand financial statements and key performance indicators
- The basics of ESG—environmental, social and governance—coverage

Selling Bonds

After its IPO (see chapter 2), sales at Sip Corp. rose every quarter for three years.

Over lunch one day, an analyst who followed Sip told a reporter from the business desk at the *Foodland Times* that he had heard the energy-drinks maker may be planning to expand.

The reporter called Chief Executive Officer Jameel Smith directly. Smith confirmed that Sip planned to build another factory at a cost of about F$100 million.

"How will you fund the project?" the reporter asked.

"Good question," Smith said. "We're probably going to sell bonds."

"Why not sell more shares?" the reporter asked.

"We thought about it, but that would reduce or dilute the value of the existing shares," Smith said. "In other words, if there were twice as many shares in circulation, the profit of each share would be halved."

"Okay, I understand, but why don't you borrow money from a bank?" the reporter asked.

Smith said he wanted to diversify his funding sources. Besides, he said, raising money from bonds would probably be cheaper than the interest rate on a loan from a bank.

"Where will you sell these bonds?" the reporter asked.

"Another good question," Smith said. "The plan is to sell them in Supplyland, which has a 'deep' bond market. In other words, there are lots of buyers and sellers of bonds there so it should be easier to raise the money we need."

What is a Bond?

A bond is an instrument used by a company or government to borrow money. Imagine a bond to be like a certificate carrying a promise. The borrower promises to pay the investor an interest rate over the life of the bond and promises to repay the principal sum to the holder of the bond when it matures.

A bond has an intrinsic value, known as the face value. A company or government that sells bonds is known as the issuer of the debt. When you buy bonds, you are lending money to the issuer. In return, you get an interest rate, known as the coupon rate. That's why a bond is also called a fixed-income security because investors know the coupon rate that they will earn is fixed and won't change.

How Sip Sold Its Bonds

Sip hired investment banks to **manage** and **underwrite** a F$100 million bond sale in Supplyland in the same way that it appointed Foodland Bank and other banks to manage its initial public offering. Sip said it would repay the money in 10 years.

The banks told Sip's management that they could sell bonds in two ways—via a **private placement** or a **public issue.**

In a private placement, the bonds are sold to select investors such as mutual funds, insurance companies and pension funds.

In a public issue, the bonds are sold to retail, or individual, investors as well.

Sip's management decided on a public offering.

The banks gauged the interest among investors for Sip's bonds. They then prepared an **offering memorandum**, also known as a **prospectus**, that provided details about Sip's businesses, the financial and legal risks of investing, details of any existing debt, the amount to be raised, the interest rate and other relevant information. The banks submitted the document to the financial regulator in Supplyland, the country where the bonds would be sold.

The prospectus contained a lot of jargon that the *Foodland Times* reporter who followed Sip wasn't familiar with. He talked with Michelle Chua, managing director and market strategist at Teaville-based Toe Stock Broking Co., to understand the process.

Chua urged the reporter to think about a bond's **face value**. Let's say the face value of each bond is S$100. It's denominated in Supplyland's currency because Sip will sell the bonds in that country.

Assume that the value of the Foodland and Supplyland currencies are the same—S$1 equals F$1. So if Sip wants to raise F$100 million in Supplyland's bond market, it can sell, for example, S$1 million in bonds to 100 investors.

In return for investors' money, Sip will offer them an interest rate, known as the **coupon rate**. This coupon rate is expressed as a percentage of the bond's face value and will be paid every year to investors until the bond's maturity.

When the bond matures in 10 years, Sip will repay the face value, sometimes called **par value**, to the bondholder.

Two main factors influence the coupon rate of a bond—the prevailing level of interest rates in the economy and the perceived risk that the borrower won't be able to repay the face value of the bond, an event known as a **default**.

If interest rates are high, the company will have to pay a higher coupon rate to entice investors.

How likely a company is to default is reflected in the **corporate bond ratings** given to it by an external ratings company. In Businessworld, the largest ratings company is ABC Ratings Co.

Sip gets a high rating from ABC Ratings, meaning it's likely to repay its debt, but Supplyland's government has an even higher rating on its own debt. A year ago, Supplyland's government borrowed money for 10 years by selling a so-called **sovereign bond** at a coupon rate of 2 percent a year.

Sip also plans to issue a 10-year bond, but its coupon rate will be double that of the sovereign bond, or 4 percent a year. Companies almost always pay investors more to buy their bonds than governments do because they are perceived as riskier.

Sip sells the bond at the face value of S$100, which is now also the **issue price**. An investor who buys the bond and holds it until maturity will earn S$4 interest a year. When the bond matures in 10 years, Sip will pay the investor the S$4 coupon and return the original S$100.

But let's assume that over time, Sip's financial condition weakens, and one of its original investors decides to sell his bonds. A new investor, investor B, who believes in Sip's long-term prospects, agrees to buy these bonds from the original investor for S$80.

Just like a stock, the price of a bond can change at any time. But the coupon rate on a bond is **fixed**. So from now on, investor B will receive the annual 4 percent coupon rate from Sip on the basis of the original S$100 par value.

But remember, investor B bought a S$100 bond for S$80. So, in effect, investor B is actually getting a higher interest rate because he is earning the same 4 percent coupon rate even after buying the bond at a cheaper price.

To calculate how much investor B effectively earns, we divide the coupon by the price at which he bought the bond. This is called the **yield**. In this example, in simple terms, it would be S$4 divided by S$80, or 5 percent. At the end of the maturity, investor B will also receive the principal, or face value, of S$100.

Let's say Sip's financial condition improves, and its bond prices are now rising. Investor B decides to sell the bond for S$120 and make a profit.

Another investor, investor C, sees value in buying the bond at S$120 given Sip's booming sales. In simple terms, the yield would now be the S$4 annual coupon payment divided by the S$120 purchase price, which is 3.33 percent.

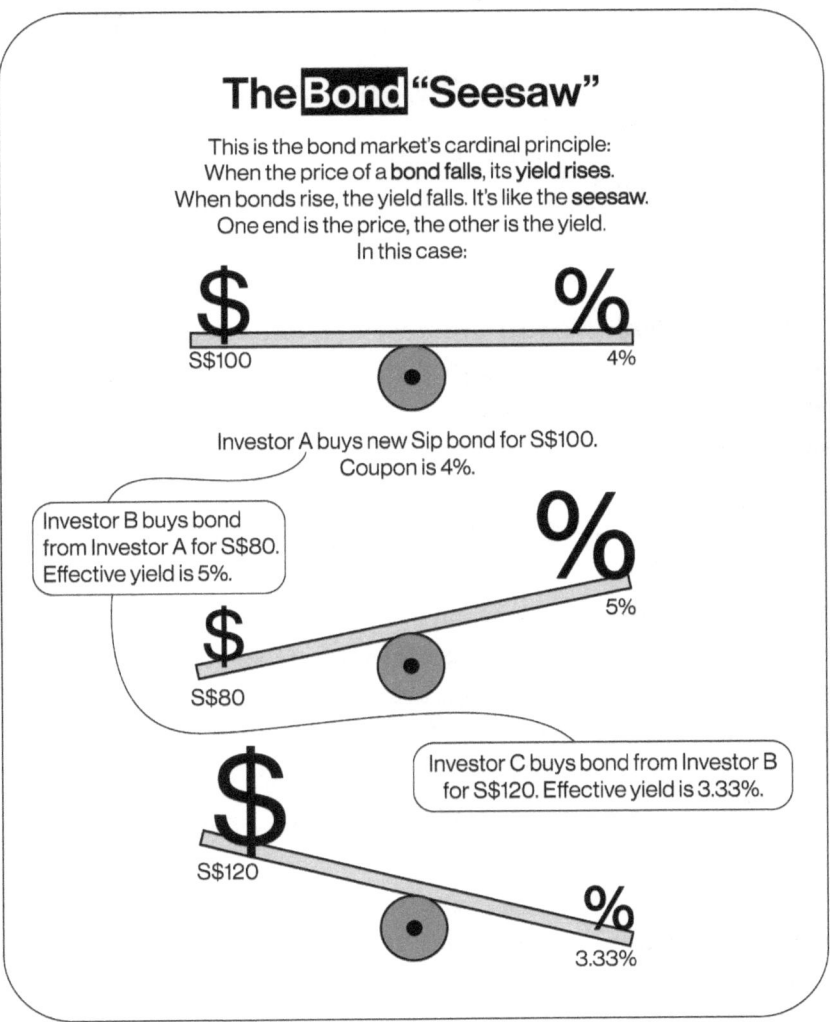

FIGURE 3.1 The bond "seesaw."

How and Why Are Companies Rated?

Investors want to get a sense of a company's ability to repay its debt, known as its **creditworthiness**.

> **INTEL**
> Companies that plan to borrow money by selling bonds get a rating from credit ratings agencies such as ABC Ratings Co. In the real world, the most prominent are Moody's Investors Service, S&P Global Ratings and Fitch Ratings. These ratings companies give grades to borrowers based on their cash flow, assets and liabilities. The borrowers usually pay the ratings companies for this service.

There are 10 **investment grades** and 10 **non-investment grades**, also known as "junk." The higher the credit rating, the better the creditworthiness of a company and the cheaper it is for the company to borrow money in the bond market.

How Do Bond Investors Make Money?

Investors make money in two ways—from higher bond prices or higher yields. When bond prices surge past the level that they bought the notes for, investors could sell the bonds and cash out. Alternatively, bond investors seek higher yields by buying bonds whose price is lower than their face value.

Why Do Journalists Track Corporate Bonds?

Business and financial media pay more attention to company share-price movements than to corporate bonds. The general public often buys shares and rarely buys corporate bonds. Yet debt usually gives a clearer picture of a company's financial health.

Journalists typically focus on the yield when writing about bonds. Changes in bond yields, caused by buying or selling bonds, are often the starting point for a bigger story. In the case of junk bonds, meaning bonds issued by companies that have either defaulted or are struggling financially, the focus is normally on bond prices. Because these issuers are risky, investors are compensated with higher interest rates. That's why junk bonds are also called high-yield bonds.

> Changes in bond yields reflect investor perceptions of a company's risk. When a company's yields are climbing, for example, it means an overwhelming number of investors are selling the company's bonds at lower prices. This could be the result of a perceived deterioration in the company's ability to repay its debt, either because its profit is falling or because the company has borrowed too much money. A higher yield could also mean that some investors are demanding a higher interest rate to buy that company's bond.

Yield to maturity shows the yield an investor would expect to earn until maturity if he or she were to buy the bond today.

Changes in yields also reflect changes in prevailing **economic conditions**. You will learn more about this in chapter 4.

How to Write About Corporate Bonds

When a story says "Bonds rose," it is referring to a gain in **bond prices**, not yields. When referring to yields, a reporter should specify that **bond yields** climbed or fell.

Companies usually don't issue just one bond. They borrow money from investors in different countries, for different rates and for varying lengths of time, depending on their needs and borrowing conditions. Reporters need to find a bond that trades more than others and is representative of the company's performance. This is called a **benchmark bond**.

The benchmark bond is usually large—hundreds of millions or billions of dollars. It has a maturity date that's at least five years in the future and has a fixed (rather than a floating) coupon rate.

When mentioning this bond in a story, reporters should include the coupon rate and the maturity date to avoid confusing it with the company's other bonds. For example, let's say Phonz Inc., the Supplyland phonemaker, issues a bond maturing in 10 years with a 3 percent coupon rate.

Table 3.1 shows the performance of that Phonz benchmark bond in early October one year.

TABLE 3.1 Phonz Bond Performance

Date	Last Price (S$)	Yield to Maturity (%)
Oct. 1	106.413	2.823
Oct. 2	106.420	2.820
Oct. 3	106.443	2.815
Oct. 4	106.588	2.785

The first column after the date shows Phonz's bond prices. It tells investors how far above or below the S$100 face value the bond is trading. The second column shows the yield. Notice that **when prices rise, the yield moves in the opposite direction**.

In this case, the bond's last price is S$106.588, which means it is above its face value of S$100. The yield is 2.785 percent, which is below the 3 percent coupon rate.

Here's the headline, lead and a paragraph of details published in a story about Phonz's bonds on Oct. 4, explaining *why* the yield fell. The subsequent paragraph offers details and data that support the lead. These details can be inserted in the narrative wherever it makes sense.

Phonz Bonds Rise After Phonemaker Posts Record Full-Year Profit

Phonz Inc.'s bonds rose after Supplyland's largest phonemaker posted its highest-ever full-year profit.

Details paragraph:
> The yield on Phonz's 3 percent bonds maturing in 10 years fell three basis points to 2.79 percent this week, according to Carsburg Bondprice Corp.

Note about the details paragraph:
- **100 basis points = 1 percentage point.** In the example above, the yield fell three basis points—to 2.79 percent from 2.82 percent. Although the yield is listed to three decimal points—2.785 percent—most publications round the number up or down to two decimal points. In this case, that's 2.79 percent.

Understanding the Spread

The gap, or difference, between the yield of any two bonds is called the **spread**. Usually, this means comparing the yield of a corporate bond with a government bond that matures around the same time.

In Sip's case, the spread is 2 percentage points, or 200 basis points, because Sip's yield is 4 percent and the Supplyland sovereign bond with a similar maturity date is 2 percent.

PRO TIP

Writing about bond spreads is a way to reinforce the theme of a corporate bond story. The spread is a gauge of risk perceptions. A widening spread means more risk. A narrowing spread suggests the company is perceived as being less risky than previously.

Here's an example:

Date	Sip's Yield	Supplyland's Yield	Spread
Dec. 3	4.66	1.65	301
Dec. 4	4.66	1.62	304
Dec. 5	4.66	1.58	308
Dec. 6	4.63	1.52	311
Dec. 7	4.68	1.50	318

Sip's 10-year bonds fell on Dec. 7 as the yield spread against Supplyland's debt with a similar maturity widened to a two-month high.

The spread is basically the extra yield investors demand to hold one bond over another bond. It shows the difference in the cost of borrowing and whether that difference is widening or narrowing.

The reporter wrote the following:

Headline:

Sip Bonds Drop Most in a Month After Company Cuts Sales Forecast

Lead:

Sips bonds fell the most in a month after the energy-drinks maker slashed its sales forecast for next year.

Details paragraph:

The yield on Sip's 4 percent bond maturing in 10 years gained five basis points to 4.68 percent, according to Carsburg Bondprice Corp. The premium—the extra yield investors demand to hold Sip's bond above Supplyland debt with a similar maturity—widened to 318 basis points from 311 basis points before the sales guidance.

Debt is often the best indicator of a company's health and future prospects. After a company announces a major corporate action, such as an acquisition, the departure of a CEO or a change in dividend, check the following:

1. Whether the magnitude of the yield move is significant
2. Whether the spread with the sovereign bond has widened or narrowed

YOUR TURN 3.1 The following table shows the spread between Inject Inc.'s 2.3% bonds maturing in November 2032 and Netland government's bonds of a similar maturity. Inject is a pharmaceuticals company in Supplyland but it issued these foreign-currency bonds in Netland. Write a paragraph about the spread on July 23.

Date	Inject's Yield	Netland's Yield	Spread
July 13	0.857	2.062	120.54
July 16	0.828	2.032	120.39
July 17	0.823	2.001	117.75
July 18	0.786	1.951	116.50
July 19	0.805	1.968	116.25
July 20	0.758	1.922	116.39
July 23	0.758	1.912	115.46

Share Split

Sip's successes sent its shares soaring.

So much so that Smith, Ogawa and the rest of the management board felt that the company's share price had become too expensive for small investors. The board decided to split the shares, making it easier for a broader range of investors to buy and sell them.

Sip's shares were split at a 2-for-1 ratio. This meant all shareholders received two shares for every one they owned.

After a stock is split, the total **value** of the shares held by a shareholder remains the same. But share prices generally rise after a split because they're cheaper to own.

The *Foodland Times* reported:

Sip to Split Stock After Shares Jumped 85 Percent Since IPO

YOUR TURN 3.2 Imagine today is Aug. 15. Write a headline and two paragraphs based on the following excerpt from a Wear Inc. press release:

> **Wear Inc. Announces 2-for-1 Stock Split**
>
> Wear Inc., the biggest clothing company in Supplyland, announces that it will split its common shares on the basis of two new common shares for each one old common share. All shareholders of record on Aug. 23 will be entitled to the stock split.
>
> Wear Inc. currently has 8,732,822 common shares issued and outstanding, which will be increased to 17,465,644 common shares after the stock split.
>
> The stock split is intended to create additional liquidity and attract a broad range of investors.
>
> Shareholders do not need to take any action with respect to the stock split. Wear's transfer agent will send owners of common shares an advice letter in lieu of a share certificate, which will represent the additional number of common shares to be received as a result of the stock split.
>
> There will be no effective change in our dividend forecast.

Mergers and Acquisitions

Sip was flush with cash from its booming sales and decided it needed to look beyond energy drinks to keep growing. After examining a lot of companies, the executives and directors decided to buy Veggi Co., a vegan company in Foodland.

Sip's board wrote to Veggi's management, expressing its desire to buy all Veggi's shares for F$4 a share. At the time, the shares were trading at F$3.20 each.

Veggi's board agreed to be taken over.

The two companies issued a press release, saying Sip would buy 100 percent of Veggi for F$4 a share. The merger is a win-win for both companies, the release said.

When one company buys another company, there are five main areas to consider:

1. The value of the deal
2. The motivation for the transaction
3. The control of the merged entity
4. The ramifications for both companies
5. The consequences for competitors

A reporter can value a deal in two ways: the **equity value** and the **enterprise** or **transaction value**.

The equity value is the price at which the acquirer buys the shares of the target company. The enterprise or transaction value is the equity value plus the debt of the target company.

Business journalists usually focus on the equity value. **The total equity value equals the offer price per share multiplied by the number of outstanding shares of the target company.**

Here's how the *Foodland Times* reporter calculated the value of the deal:

Sip's offer price: F$4 a share.

The reporter called Veggi to find out how many shares were outstanding. There were 5 million.

The total equity value = F$4 × 5 million = F$20 million.

The *Foodland Times* headline was:

Sip to Buy Veggi for F$20 Million to Expand Into Vegan Products

The above is an example of a cash-only offer.

It was also a **friendly takeover** because the board of the target company, Veggi, agreed to be taken over.

When a target company refuses a takeover plan, the prospective buyer can approach the target company's shareholders directly with an offer to buy the company. This is called a **hostile takeover**.

Note that the press release used the word "merger" and said that it was a "win-win" for both companies. This is common. But beware: **True mergers rarely happen.** One company almost always buys another.

The winner here was Sip, although many Veggi shareholders were happy to sell because they received F4$ a share, which was 25 percent more than the $F3.20 a share at which Veggi was trading the night before the deal was announced. This is known as the **premium**. On the other hand, when a sale happens for less than the stock price, it's called a **discount**.

Later that year, Sip's board proposed a takeover to the board of Snackable Inc., Foodland's largest snacks maker.

Sip's management decided to buy Snackable's shares by offering its own shares rather than cash.

Sip offered 0.5 of its shares for every Snackable share. This is called the **exchange ratio**.

YOUR TURN 3.3

Web Co. announces an agreement to buy Driverless Inc. Web's offer is N$10 a share in cash and 0.7 of a Web share for every Driverless share. Web's shares closed a day earlier at N$60. Driverless shares closed at N$50. Driverless has 1.123 billion shares outstanding.

1. How much is Web offering to pay per share for Driverless?

2. What is the total offer price?

3. What premium or discount is Web offering?

At the time of the announcement, Sip's shares were trading at F$20 a share.

To calculate the value of the stock-only offer, the reporter had to establish Sip's offer price per share.

Offer price per share = buyer's share price multiplied by the exchange ratio.

So, Sip's offer price for every Snackable share = F$20 × 0.5 = F$10.

The reporter called Snackable to find out how many shares were outstanding. There were 2.2 million.

The total equity value of the deal: F$10 × 2,200,000 = F$22 million.

The *Foodland Times* headline was:

Sip Offers to Buy Snackable in Deal Valued at F$22 Million

When an investor buys a significant stake in a target company, keep an eye on the open offer that normally follows. In many countries, an acquirer must make an open offer, an invitation to the shareholders of the target company to sell their shares at a particular price. The objective is to give the target company's shareholders an exit option, since there is a change in the control of their company.

Buybacks

A few years later, Sip's Smith was concerned that his company could find itself as the target of a takeover. By then, Sip had amassed a lot of cash. It had been putting money aside from its profit each quarter rather than increasing its dividend to shareholders.

Smith proposed to the company's board that Sip buy back some of its shares. This would help reduce the supply of outstanding shares and hence boost the company's earnings per share, or EPS.

The board approved buying back 43,000 shares for a total not exceeding F$35 million. The shares represented 10 percent of the share capital of the company.

The *Foodland Times* reported:

Sip Approves F$35 Million Share Buyback to Thwart Takeover Risk
Sip Corp. plans to buy back 10 percent of its shares for about F$35 million as its board tries to fend off private equity companies that want to purchase the energy drinks maker.

PRO TIP

Companies buy back or repurchase their shares to boost their earnings per share.

In press releases on buybacks, focus on:

1. How much the company plans to spend to repurchase the shares
2. What percentage of the equity capital the company is buying back
3. What price the company is paying to buy back each share

Company shares usually rise after a buyback is announced. A buyback signals that a company is confident in its performance. Also, by buying back shares, there will be fewer shares outstanding, which means the earnings per share, or EPS, should rise.

Dividends

Some institutional investors lost interest in Sip because of stagnant dividend earnings from the company. After four years of paying out the same annual dividend to shareholders, Sip's board increased it to F$0.11 a share from F$0.10 a share.

This record 10 percent increase was designed to appease shareholders. It meant that their **total return**—the price change plus the reinvestment of the higher dividends—would be higher than what they would receive from most of Sip's competitors. Sip's stock was trading at F$18.

The *Foodland Times* wrote:

Headline:

Sip Boosts Dividend for First Time in Five Years by Record 10 Percent

Lead:

Sip Corp. increased its dividend for the first time in five years after major investors threatened to sell their stake in the energy-drinks maker over stagnant payouts.

Details paragraph:

The record 10 percent jump gives Sip shareholders an indicated yield of 6 percent, the largest payout among companies in Foodland. Sip will pay shareholders 11 Foodland cents a share, up from 10 cents, the company said Tuesday.

Dividend, Ex-Dividend and Dividend Yield

A **dividend** is the proportion of earnings or profit that a company gives to its shareholders. It can be issued as cash or stock. A company is not obliged to pay a dividend. Dividends are usually paid quarterly or semiannually.

When a company announces a dividend, it fixes a record date. All shareholders who are registered as of that date become eligible for a payout based on their holdings.

Two days before the record date, the stock goes **ex-dividend** — that is, the dividend is factored into the price of the stock. For a shareholder to be eligible to receive a dividend, he or she must own the company's shares before the stock goes ex-dividend.

In the above example, when Sip's stock goes ex-dividend, it automatically falls by the amount of the dividend payout, or 11 Foodland cents.

Investors who want to earn an income from dividend payouts focus on what is known as the **dividend yield or indicated yield**. Expressed as a percentage, the dividend yield shows the annual cash returns an investor could expect to receive from dividends over the next year by owning one share of a company. It's calculated by dividing the most-recent annual dividend paid per share, by the price per share, multiplied by 100.

Earnings

It's mid-April in Foodland and the first-quarter "earnings season" is in full swing.

In most countries, the earnings season is a month-long period that begins about two weeks after the end of each quarter. This is when companies report how they performed during the quarter in what's known as an **income statement**. Companies also release a **balance sheet**, a snapshot of a company's assets and liabilities, and a **cash flow statement**, which shows cash inflows and outflows during a specific period. These are required by law for all listed companies. However, companies disclose different kinds of financial information depending on their home country.

The business year, or the **fiscal year**, of many companies differs, too. Most follow the January-to-December calendar year. Hence, their first quarter is Jan. 1 to March 31, and so on. Some begin their fiscal year in other months. There's no set rule. When comparing companies, it's important to know when the fiscal year begins to avoid making incorrect assumptions.

Some companies only release financial statements twice a year, rather than four times. This depends on the country's financial regulator.

Sip Corp., the Foodland energy-drinks maker, follows the calendar year and reports its earnings four times a year. It said first-quarter profit doubled to F$26 million from a year earlier. Revenue grew 14 percent to F$68 million.

Note that "profit" comes in many forms, so it's important to specify what kind—operating profit; earnings before interest, taxes, depreciation and amortization (ebitda); pretax profit; profit before extraordinary items and so on. Most business journalists want to know **the top line**, which is called revenue, sales or turnover, and **the bottom line**, which is net income. A familiar form of net income that many analysts and journalists look for on the income statement is called **net income attributable to common shareholders, adjusted.**

When comparing figures, always look at the year-earlier numbers, not the preceding quarter or half-year. In other words, compare this year's second quarter with the second quarter last year.

In Sip's case, 16 analysts in Foodland and elsewhere closely tracked the company's financial performance. Their average estimate for net income was F$24 million, which was F$2 million less than what the company reported.

The *Foodland Times* reporter prepared for Sip's first-quarter earnings by reading previous Sip earnings statements and by talking to company officials and analysts. To ensure the *Foodland Times* published a story before its rivals, the reporter prepared three stories. These were based on whether net income would be higher or lower than analysts' estimates and why. These story templates captured three likely scenarios:

Sip Profit Doubles as New Energy Snacks, Vegetables Spur Sales

Sip Profit Beats Estimates as Energy Snacks, Vegetables Power Sales

Sip Profit Misses Estimates as Customers Shun Energy Snacks, Vegetables

Seconds after Sip's announcement, the *Foodland Times* published the second headline and story—*Sip Profit Beats Estimates*—on its website. Its affiliated television station, FTV, ran a banner headline on the screen during a news program. The reporter started to update the story, adding details from the earnings press release and more comments from officials and analysts.

Suddenly, he stopped typing. The reporter noted that Sip shares were tumbling despite the positive earnings news. Within minutes, they had dropped 6 percent, the biggest decline in four months. Why?

The best business journalists anticipate the news. The reporter immediately wrote the word "guidance" in the press release's search box to see whether the company had made a forecast or outlook. Low down in the press release, he found a short paragraph projecting Sip's sales and profits for the second quarter. Both numbers were lower than those of the current quarter and below those of the second quarter a year earlier.

The reporter switched gears. The story was no longer a positive one. He wrote a new headline and short narrative, which FTV also picked up and broadcast.

Sip Shares Plunge as Energy-Drinks Maker Forecasts Lower Profit, Sales
> Sip Corp. shares fell the most in four months after the energy-drinks maker forecast that sales and profit will drop in the second quarter.

Why was the company expecting a weaker performance? The press release didn't answer that question. The reporter sent text messages to contacts and made a couple of quick phone calls.

One analyst told him that "the competitive environment for energy drinks is becoming increasingly severe." Another said that Sip's advertisements weren't particularly popular with many people who usually bought the beverage. Within 30 minutes, he was ready to write another breaking news story. Here's the second and third paragraphs:

> The projected decline stems from an increase in competition for energy drinks and the failure of a multimillion-dollar advertising campaign promoting the beverages, according to analysts who follow the stock.
>
> Sip Chief Executive Officer Jameel Smith didn't reply to two text messages asking for comment. A Sip spokesperson declined to comment.

It was a typical earnings day. The reporter's careful preparation had yielded one clear story, but this was quickly overtaken by events. By switching to a second and then a third theme, the reporter stayed on top of the story and served both *Foodland Times*'s readers and FTV's viewers.

An earnings story should answer these basic questions:

1. Did the company make a profit or loss?
2. Did the profit rise or fall?
3. Did the loss widen or narrow?
4. Did these numbers beat or trail analysts' estimates?
5. Why?
6. What's the impact of the change in the bottom line?
7. Has revenue grown or shrunk?
8. Are costs under control or not?
9. How's the key metric for the industry doing? For example, in the case of banks, it would be the non-performing assets.

The words profit, income and earnings are synonymous. Profit is expressed in two ways — the total amount and the profit per outstanding share, known as earnings per share or EPS.

Reporters should generally focus on net income because that's the bottom line. If the company and analysts explain that another profitability metric is a more appropriate way to measure performance, be transparent in explaining why.

While focusing on net income and other metrics, analysts normally focus on "adjusted numbers" given by companies.

An adjusted net income, for example, strips out any one-time revenue or expense from the calculation. These could be items such as an extraordinary gain from the sale of real estate or a one-off tax burden that could obscure the real performance of the company in that quarter.

How to Write a Typical Earnings Story

For the lead, begin with the company name and say whether the measure of profitability you're using—usually net income—beat or lagged analysts' estimates, and why.

Or say whether profit rose or fell from the same period a year earlier. Or focus on the company's outlook for profit over the next quarter or year.

When a company posts a loss, say whether the loss widened or narrowed. **Profits increase or decrease. Losses widen or narrow.**

Add a paragraph high in the story that focuses on **what the earnings mean** to the company, investors and/or rivals. This may, for instance, answer some key questions: Can the growth be sustained? What challenges does the company face? How does the company's performance compare with that of its peers? What is the market reaction indicating? Does the profit reflect anything about the state of the economy?

When relevant, add a paragraph with **forward-looking comments** from an investor or analyst that elaborates on the theme of the story and gives a sense of what's going to happen next.

PRO TIP

Run a **keyboard search** for words in the press release like outlook, guidance or forecast. Also search for words like jobs, hiring, concern, risk and restructure. These are often of interest for readers because they will influence the company's future business.

Look for the share-price reaction because the direction will help you identify the real story. For example, sometimes investors may focus on sales rather than net income. So don't blindly lead with net income in every earnings story. Follow the money!

PRO TIP

How to prepare for company earnings:

1. Read the company's press releases from the previous two quarters to see where the key numbers are typically mentioned.
2. Go over the earnings coverage of the past two quarters to get a sense of the focus of the stories and issues facing the company.
3. Check for any recent corporate developments, including management changes, lawsuits, contracts won or lost, takeovers and job cuts.
4. Find out analysts' consensus estimate on earnings, revenue and earnings per share.

Add a paragraph with details, which mentions the specific profitability numbers and what analysts estimated. Make sure to add what kind of company you're writing about. If it's well known, this information doesn't need to be high in the story.

It's important to remember that **earnings statements are report cards gauging how well company executives are running the business.** The financial results are a direct consequence of decisions made by top officials, such as acquisitions, opening or closing of factories, price cuts or hikes and more.

In short, every earnings announcement provides an opportunity to tell a story. Don't just reproduce numbers from the press release.

YOUR TURN
3.4

Write a four-paragraph earnings story about Fizz Co., a maker of carbonated drinks in Foodland, based on the following details about the company's fourth-quarter earnings, which were announced in an emailed statement:

Fizz Co. said fourth-quarter net income fell 3% to F$622 million, or 23 cents a share, from F$641 million, or 25 cents, a year earlier.

The results missed the average forecast of 24 cents a share of 19 analysts surveyed by the *Foodland Times*.

It was the first decline in Fizz's earnings in six quarters.

Costs to develop new drinks and advertising campaigns reduced earnings by F$25 million.

"Investors don't like it when earnings miss guidance," said Dun Paris, a senior analyst at FFF Securities in Teaville, Foodland. Paris rates the stock "buy."

On a conference call with analysts after the earnings announcement, Chief Executive Officer Priyanka Spirit said new low-sugar drinks such as Van Fizz and Cool Fizz were a big hit with teenagers and young adults.

Sales rose 8.1% to F$5.18 billion, the biggest percentage gain in 10 years. Fizz had forecast a 4% increase in sales.

"Our strategy is being well executed, as everyone can see from the sales results," Spirit said on the call. "The fizz is back."

Fizz shares surged 10% to F$5.50 from F$5. That was the biggest percentage gain in four years.

Fizz spent F$100 million in the past two years developing the new products as sales of Fizz Classic and Slim Fizz stagnated. The spending reduced earnings.

Park Won Wei, a money manager with Fund City, Bankland-based Get Rich Asset Management Co., which holds 6 million Fizz shares, said: "We waited a long time for Fizz's new products to finally bear fruit. Sales will only get better from here."

Understanding Financial Statements

Listed companies usually release three financial statements every quarter or half-year: an income statement, a balance sheet and a cash-flow statement. Each one can help reporters understand how a company is performing.

PRO TIP

Company reporters typically need to know the general **valuation** methods, or **key performance indicators (KPIs)** by which all companies are judged. These include profit and revenue growth, profit margins, sales per employee and the price/earnings ratio.

They also need to know the performance indicators that are **specific to an industry**. For example, a popular airline metric is called revenue passenger miles (RPM) while technology companies look at research and development spending as a percentage of net sales.

Telecommunications and media companies calculate the average revenue per unit/user (ARPU) and the churn rate, which shows the percentage of subscribers quitting. Ecommerce companies view the average order value (AOV).

Some items to consider.
In the ***income statement***, check:

- **Revenue growth.** How much did the business grow—or contract—in the period compared with a year earlier? It is the most fundamental thing to look at while analyzing a company's financial performance.
- **Net income growth.** By what percentage was net income higher or lower than in the previous period? What contributed to the change in

the bottom line? When was the last time net income rose or fell this much?
- **Operating costs.** Which specific expenses are growing faster than others? Look at the breakdown of costs in areas such as marketing, administrative, research and development and labor costs.
- **Non-operating costs.** Check interest expenses, foreign-exchange gains and losses, taxes, and gains or losses due to things like job cuts or factory closures.
- **Operating margin.** This closely watched metric reflects operating profit (operating income) divided by revenue multiplied by 100. A wider operating margin may show that the company is reducing its raw material and labor costs. Or vice versa.
- **Profit margin.** Net income divided by revenue multiplied by 100. This shows how much profit a company is making as a percentage of its revenue. For example, if revenue is $100 million and net income is $5 million, the profit margin is 5 percent. Investors want to know whether the margins are widening or narrowing and how they compare with those of competitors.
- **Diluted earnings per share.** Most shareholders are interested in this profitability metric, which shows net income divided by the total number of outstanding shares. Diluted EPS takes into account all the shares issued by the company, such as stock options given to employees that may not yet have been exercised by their owners. (See chapter 9 for calculation of EPS.)

In the ***balance sheet***, check:

- **Cash and near cash.** Near cash (cash equivalents) means short-term investments that can be readily converted into cash. Together, these show the amount of money the company has on hand to spend, if necessary.
- **Net fixed assets.** Growth in net fixed assets shows the company is creating capacity for future growth. The value of these assets is derived after providing for **depreciation**. This is an expense that reduces the

value of assets because of wear and tear. For companies that create knowledge-based or "smart" products, the equivalent of net fixed assets is called **intangible assets**.

- **Long-term borrowings.** Borrowing trends offer insight into a company's performance. When a company borrows *less*, it may suggest it has adequate cash to invest for future growth. If the trend is increasing, check why.
- **Accounts receivable and notes.** The money that a company is owed by its dealers and vendors. When receivables jump, a company may be facing problems collecting money it is owed. Or perhaps the company isn't performing well and there's declining demand for its products.
- **Inventories.** The value of the goods that haven't yet been sold. Growth in inventories often suggests slowing demand for the company's products. When inventories are low, it may mean the company is unable to keep up with demand.
- **Accounts payable.** The money the company owes its suppliers. When accounts payable increase, the company has bargaining power to delay payments. Alternatively, it may mean the company doesn't have enough money to pay its suppliers.
- **Total debt/equity.** This shows how leveraged a company is—how much debt it has in relation to its equity.
- **Current ratio** or **liquidity ratio.** This shows a company's ability to pay its short-term obligations. Divide current assets (assets that can be turned into cash in a year) by current liabilities (debt maturing in a year). The result should be at least 1. If the ratio falls below 1, check whether the company is facing difficulties.

In the *cash-flow statement*, check:

- **Cash from operations.** This shows how much cash the company has generated from its core business and should be a positive number. A lot of investors look at this metric because it shows whether the company is generating enough cash to invest in the business. Operating cash flows and net income usually move in tandem.

- **Cash from investing.** This item tracks cash flow to buy or sell assets. The number should be negative, especially when companies are growing and investing in fixed assets.
- **Cash from financing.** This item records cash generated from stock sales and debt. When a company isn't generating enough cash from operations, it may need to borrow money. The number becomes negative if dividend payments and loan repayments outpace security issuance.
- **Return on equity.** This is useful to compare the profitability of a company with that of other firms in the same industry. It shows how much profit a company generates with the money shareholders have invested. ROE = Net income/shareholder's equity.

ESG Data

After Sip Corp. posted its first-quarter earnings, Chief Executive Officer Smith held a conference call with analysts who track the company's performance. A few journalists, including the business reporter at the *Foodland Times*, joined the call on the condition that they could listen and take notes but not participate. This is routine during the "earnings season" in many countries.

During the call, an analyst asked Smith how Sip's plans to reduce greenhouse-gas emissions and to cut the amount of plastic in its energy-drink bottles were proceeding.

Smith was ebullient. "We're greener than ever!" he said. "Our carbon emissions are 8 percent lower than a year ago. As for plastic, we're currently testing several types of bottles that contain far less plastic. I have high hopes of rolling at least one of these out this year."

The *Foodland Times* reporter decided to look into these and other environmental, social and governance (ESG) issues at Sip. Companies increasingly collect ESG data and set ESG targets. In turn, investors often look at companies' ESG results to gauge their sustainability and ethical outlook. The data differ depending on the industry.

Environmental data usually include electricity and water use, carbon dioxide emissions, hazardous waste disposal, energy imports, paper consumption, compliance with government environmental regulations and resource conservation.

Social data collected by companies often include employee turnover, the percentage of women, minorities and unionized labor in the workforce, donations to local communities, the extent of volunteerism and workplace discrimination.

Governance data include the transparency of accounting methods, the number of independent directors on a company's board, litigation analysis, the avoidance of illegal practices and other topics related to how well a company is governed.

ESG comparisons are difficult. Every company likes to say it's "green," transparent and nondiscriminatory. Business journalists need to be vigilant—and skeptical—when reporting these figures. There's a real risk of misleading readers and viewers by reporting the corporate hype.

The *Foodland Times* reporter decided to focus on one small part of the ESG issue after interviewing Sip's head of sustainability and talking to analysts who follow the company. Here's the first five paragraphs of her breaking news story:

Sip to Sell All Soft Drinks in Fully Recycled Plastic Bottles

Sip Corp. plans to sell all its soft drinks in fully recycled bottles starting next year as the Foodland beverage giant tries to reduce its environmental footprint.

The shift will cut the use of new plastic by 500 tons a year, according to Sip officials. Plastic packaging for the bottles will consist of entirely recycled material, except for caps and labels.

Sip is responding to a growing consumer backlash against plastic pollution after the StopWasteNow coalition named the company as one of Businessworld's worst contaminators.

The new bottles are the result of a Sip-patented technology that will be used to recycle polyethylene terephthalate, or PET, plastics, Sip's head of sustainability, Kae Kristal, said in an interview.

"Plastic is not the enemy," she said. Most plastic packaging until now has been single-use. From next year, that equation will change at Sip, she said.

YOUR TURN 3.5: Choose two of the scenarios below and outline in no more than 300 words each how you would approach reporting and writing the stories for an international news organization. Be as specific as possible.

An influential non-governmental organization accuses an international clothing company of exploiting workers.

A whistleblower sends you a series of detailed messages alleging accounting irregularities at a supermarket chain.

A 60-year-old male chief executive officer at a leading company is arrested for alleged sexual harassment of women over the past decade.

Your news organization receives in the mail some documents that appear to show that a small energy company is not disposing of hazardous wastes in line with government regulations.

The Final Word

Company reporters must **prepare for the routine**: dividends and divestitures, earnings and events, annual general meetings and other **corporate actions**. Yet it's usually unexpected developments that become the top news of the day.

The company journalist's job is to **anticipate and uncover surprises** and to write compelling narratives that are both readable and have an impact. It's a job that requires the reporter to become an **expert** on small groups of companies or industries and to **build sources** who, over time, can keep her in the loop and point the way to scoops.

Remember that the stories journalists write are ultimately about human beings and their very real human motivations. Behind every corporate strategy there will usually be competing interests. Smart journalists dig deep to get to know the personalities behind the brands. They understand the relationships, alliances and conflicts that arise day to day.

By building rapport and trust with sources within a business, these reporters are able to keep on top of the twists, turns and tensions that make covering companies so exciting.

4

• • • •

The Country Story

The First Word

Gross domestic product. Inflation. Jobs and unemployment. Retail sales. Trade. Business and consumer confidence. House prices.

These are some of the indicators that business journalists keep a close eye on when covering local, regional and national economies. Yet telling the country story is far more than dry economic numbers. **Every piece of data is an opportunity to tell a story about what's happening in an economy and how it affects individuals, companies and governments.**

What, for example, do rising consumer prices mean to the average household? What effect does the closing or construction of a factory have on the spending habits of a community? What does the aging of the workforce mean for a community? Why should individuals care that economic growth is decelerating?

This chapter examines these and other economic themes from the perspective of Commonland, the second-largest economy in Businessworld.

You will learn the following in this chapter:

- How an economy functions
- How to write stories about a country's economy
- The importance of the Purchasing Managers Index

- The role of central banks in an economy
- The essentials of monetary and fiscal policy
- Inflation and the Consumer Price Index
- Why governments sell bonds
- The relevance of currencies in country stories
- Trade, jobs, homes and other key economic indicators
- The links between politics and economies

Measuring an Economy

Commonland is rich in natural resources such as iron ore and crude oil. Manufacturing is a major part of the economy, and the country produces everything from cars to chocolates. The nation is also home to some of Businessworld's biggest construction companies and commercial banks.

Many foreign investors have been flocking to Commonland to invest in its markets and companies. The latest are fund managers from Gasopolis Asset Management Co. in Energyland and Netland Asset Management Co.

Before the fund managers commit any money, they want to know how Commonland is performing. So they work with economists and other experts to analyze the situation through the lens of **economic indicators**.

One common indicator that measures the state of the economy is called **gross domestic product (GDP)**. It's the value (i.e., the price multiplied by the quantity) of all the goods and services produced in the country.

On April 29, Commonland's Central Statistics Office announced GDP data for the January-to-March quarter. GDP, like most data, is a **lagging economic indicator** because it shows performance in the past.

In a press statement, the statistics office announced that **real GDP** for the quarter had grown 0.4 percent from the previous quarter and was 1.8 percent higher than in the same quarter a year earlier.

In advanced economies, business journalists usually pay closest attention to the **quarter-on-quarter (QoQ)** statistics for GDP. That's because the data are **seasonally adjusted**, meaning they take into account the time of year and the number of holidays and weekends in each month. In countries where data aren't adjusted for seasonality, journalists focus on the **year-on-year (YoY)** numbers.

Focusing on quarterly changes in GDP allows journalists to see whether the economy is trending toward growth or, during periods of slowdown, **recession**. Some economists define recession as a decline in GDP for two consecutive quarters.

For other key performance indicators, such as retail sales and the Consumer Price Index, governments often provide both month-on-month (MoM) and year-on-year (YoY) data.

The Commonland government broke down the quarter-on-quarter GDP data by sector: housing contracted 0.8 percent, banking grew 0.1 percent, automobiles declined 0.2 percent, steel fell 0.3 percent and crude oil expanded 0.3 percent.

How do real GDP and nominal GDP differ?

Business journalists (and economists) focus on **real GDP** rather than nominal GDP.

GDP is the total value of all goods and services produced in a country.

Nominal GDP includes changes in production and changes in prices. Therefore, it doesn't show the real growth in the value of goods and services produced because prices may have increased and inflated the GDP, or vice versa.

Real GDP adjusts or isolates increases in prices, known as **inflation**. (When prices fall, it's called **deflation**.)

Example:

Let's say country A produces only shoes.

In year 1, it produced 1,000 pairs of shoes and sold them for $10 a pair. The GDP of country A in year 1 would be 1,000 × 10 = $10,000.

In year 2, it produced 2,000 pairs and sold them for $20 each. The GDP of country A in year 2 would be 2,000 × 20 = $40,000.

That's an increase of four times from year 1. But did the economy really increase by that magnitude?

In nominal terms, yes.

But the real GDP, which shows how productive the country really was or by how much the economy actually grew, didn't increase by that much.

That's because some of that increase in GDP in year 2 was the result of an increase in prices.

In the calculation of real GDP, economists focus only on the quantity and keep prices constant.

A simple way to calculate real GDP in year 2 would be to multiply the quantity produced in year 2 with the price of year 1.

That is, 2,000 × 10 = $20,000.

So real GDP rose 100 percent in year 2 from year 1. In other words, the size of country A's economy doubled.

Year 1 is known as the base year, or the year that is referenced for prices to calculate GDP.

At the *Commonland Express*, the reporter was ready to file a story for the website on the nation's latest GDP figures. Before the government released the numbers, she wrote short templates capturing two possible scenarios. In one, she said the data came in better than economists had forecast. The second said the data fared worse than the estimates.

As soon as the data were released, the reporter:

- Compared the new figures with previous quarters to add context about trends in the percentage growth. For example, was it the largest or the smallest quarterly growth in a certain number of quarters?
- Compared the data with economists' expectations.

The reporter noted that the 0.4 percent growth was the slowest in four quarters. She also noted that economists' **median** estimate was for the economy to expand 0.6 percent. This was based on a survey of economists at nine financial institutions, including Peak Analytics Co., Accurate Predictions Plc and Rare Insights Co.

The *Commonland Express*'s initial headline and lead provided readers with information about what happened and why.

(First Version):

Commonland Economy Grows at Weakest Pace in a Year as Housing Slumps

Commonland's economy grew at its weakest pace in a year as a drop in demand for houses hurt construction and steel businesses.

Gross domestic product rose 0.4 percent in the three months through March compared with the previous quarter, according to Commonland's Central Statistics Office. Economists had forecast a 0.6 percent gain. Housing contracted 0.8 percent and steel fell 0.3 percent.

PRO TIP

Style points to remember regarding GDP:

- Economic growth = increase in gross domestic product

- The economy expands, grows, shrinks or contracts. It doesn't rise or fall.

- Gross domestic product can rise or fall. It can expand, grow, shrink or contract.

- If the second-quarter GDP growth rate was 3% and the third quarter was 3.3%, you could write that growth accelerated or that the growth rate was higher in the third quarter than in the second quarter. You could also say that the economy expanded at a faster pace in the third quarter than in the previous three months.

- If the second-quarter GDP growth rate was 2% and the third quarter was -1%, then the economy or GDP shrank or contracted in the third quarter.

THE COUNTRY STORY • 71

YOUR TURN
it's
4.1

Smart reporters can sense the pace of economic growth several months before the official data are released. They observe consumers shopping for groceries and clothes in stores. They talk to their friends and families to gauge whether they are buying more or cutting back their online purchases. They read business stories and watch business news channels to see what kind of companies are enjoying higher profits or suffering lower sales. These decisions and actions by individuals and businesses eventually feed into the GDP data.

Based on your observations and conversations, will the next quarter show an economic expansion or contraction in your city or country? On what specifically do you base this conclusion?

The Central Bank

For the past year, Commonland's central bank, the Reserve Bank of Commonland, has been trying to revive demand in the economy. Its target was to achieve 2 percent quarter-on-quarter GDP growth.

Two key functions served by central banks are to ensure the economy is growing and to control inflation using **monetary policy**.

give me the **INTEL**

What are Monetary Policy Tools?

To control growth and inflation, central banks normally use the following tools — benchmark interest rates; open market operations; and reserve requirements (cash, statutory reserve).

Commonland's benchmark rate is called the repo or repurchase rate, which is the interest rate at which the Reserve Bank of Commonland lends money to commercial banks. In some countries, this is called the discount rate.

Growth and inflation are usually opposing forces. When an economy expands too quickly, it means consumers are demanding more and more goods and services. This stokes inflation, meaning a rise in consumer prices for those goods and services. Conversely, slowing growth or contraction leads to a decline in the inflation rate, or sometimes deflation. Deflation is negative inflation, when prices generally fall.

Central banks use monetary policy tools at their disposal to try to keep the economy growing at an optimum pace that will help generate jobs and contain inflation.

Commonland's economy was almost stagnant the previous year, and the challenge for its central bank was to revive consumer demand.

Interest rates are the most commonly used tool by central banks. When an economy expands at a pace that pushes up the inflation rate beyond levels that are comfortable for the central bank, the bank **raises key interest rates** to slow consumer borrowing from banks and tamp down demand.

Conversely, when growth slows or contracts, a central bank typically **cuts its benchmark interest rate**. The rationale is that commercial banks in turn would pass on the cheaper rates to consumers, making mortgages and car loans cheaper. The central bankers hope that cheaper borrowing costs will encourage consumers to borrow more money and spend it on houses, cars and other goods, thereby stimulating the economy.

> **Open market operations** refer to the buying and selling of government, mortgage or sometimes corporate bonds. If a central bank wants to reduce borrowing costs in an economy, it can buy government bonds, for instance, held by commercial banks, releasing cash to these banks. When this supply of cash grows, it helps lower the price of money — that is interest rates.

INTEL

Similarly, if the central bank wants to increase borrowing costs, it can sell bonds to commercial banks. This drains cash from lenders, squeezing the flow of money into the economy and increasing interest rates. Central banks use this tool when they need to take more aggressive steps to curb growth and keep inflation in check. The usual priority is to tackle inflation first.

> **INTEL**
>
> The **reserve requirements** work similarly to open market operations. Commercial banks are required to keep a certain portion of their deposits with the central bank. This money is set aside by the central bank and acts as a buffer to maintain stability and liquidity in the banking system.
>
> Central banks make decisions after assessing their **monetary policy stance**. An **accommodative stance** means the bank tries to expand the monetary supply to boost the economy when growth is slowing. A **restrictive stance** reduces the amount of money banks can lend, cutting the money supply. A **neutral stance** means the central bank is neither stimulating nor restraining economic growth.

The Reserve Bank of Commonland's eight-member monetary policy committee meets every month to discuss the state of the economy.

To spur growth, the committee cut its benchmark interest rate, or **repo rate**, by a quarter of a percentage point, or 25 basis points, every other month last year. In all, Commonland's central bank lowered this rate by 1.5 percentage points, or 150 basis points, to a record-low 1 percent.

The *Commonland Express*'s reporter updated her story with a response from business groups, context about the central bank and a quote from an economist.

(Update1):

Commonland Economy's Slower Growth Prompts Calls for More Rate Cuts

Commonland's economy expanded at its weakest pace in a year, prompting calls for the nation's central bank to take more action to stimulate growth.

Commonland's Chamber of Commerce and two smaller industry groups said the government and central bank must take more aggressive steps to revive growth in Businessworld's second-largest economy.

Gross domestic product rose 0.4 percent in the three months through March compared with the previous quarter, the country's statistics office said. Economists had forecast a 0.6 percent gain.

The Reserve Bank of Commonland slashed its benchmark rate six times last year to a record-low 1 percent. Accelerating inflation this year leaves the central bank with little scope for further cuts, according to Pankaj Castro, an economist at Peak Analytics Co. in Diversia.

"With inflation creeping up, I see a danger in simply cutting rates more and more," Castro said. "It's not going to be easy to boost consumer demand."

Commonland's two largest companies by revenue—GiantSteel Corp. and Stellarcars Co.—have both signaled that a slowdown in sales will hurt profit in the second half of the year. Commonland Construction Co. said it may build fewer homes this year because of waning demand.

Does the central bank have room to cut interest rates?

That's a key question policy makers discuss when they consider reducing the central bank's benchmark rate to boost economic growth.

The "room" we are referring to here is the inflation rate. Namely, is the inflation rate low enough that reducing the benchmark interest rate won't lead to an unsustainable acceleration in consumer prices.
Also, will it hurt the interest income that investors earn?

For example, let's say the inflation rate is 5%, and the central bank's benchmark interest rate is 9%. And assume that economic growth is slowing. In this case, there is still some space for the central bank to cut its interest rates without harming the real returns of investors. If it cuts rates by a quarter point to 8.75% to spur expansion, investors would still receive a positive return of 3.75 percentage points (8.75%-5%).

However, consider this scenario: the inflation rate is 8% and the central bank's benchmark rate is 9%. Growth is slowing and inflation is accelerating, too. In this case, the central bank will be constrained in how much it can cut rates — because it has to balance growth and inflation concerns. A cut would also mean investors aren't left with any real return, after inflation.

YOUR TURN 4.2 Write a six-paragraph story about the following GDP announcement from Bankland and the background information.

Following is the summary of Bankland's GDP data for the fourth quarter that ended on Dec. 31, compared with the third quarter. It was released by the country's statistics office on Feb. 28.

Gross Domestic Product   1.80%

By Industry		By Expenditure	
Agriculture	1.26%	Household spending	4.97%
Mining	0.94%	Government spending	0.48%
Manufacturing	1.96%	Investment	4.06%
Electricity	-1.01%	Exports	-0.39%
Construction	1.79%	Imports	-8.05%
Services	1.58%		

- 1.80% growth is the weakest in four years.

- A deadly virus, called the vipervirus, was found in central Bankland in January and spread rapidly. More than 1,000 people died as a result of the virus as of Feb. 28. Half the factories in Bankland are in the country's central region and most are shut because of the outbreak of the virus. The virus spreads through human contact.

- The median estimate for growth was 2%.

- "There is an urgent need for a concerted stimulus package," said Brian Fernandez, who helps manage B$100 million in equities at Growth Asset Management Co. in Fund City, Bankland. "Otherwise, it will be hard to arrest this slide in growth." He said first-quarter growth could drop to 0.5%. Fernandez said he expected the central bank to cut its key rate and cash reserve ratio by 50 basis points in a policy announcement on March 5. Fernandez's Growth Stocks Fund was the best-performing equity fund in the country last year.

- Minutes after the GDP data were released, Bankland central bank released a statement saying it will maintain an "accommodative monetary policy stance." It said that the easing will not be limited to lowering the benchmark rate.

- The central bank also called for greater coordination between monetary and fiscal authorities to support growth, saying the "central bank cannot be the only game in town."

- The central bank has lowered its key rate four times, by a percentage point in total, in the past six months.

- Government spending of 0.48% in the fourth quarter is the slowest pace in three years. That's because a slowing economy has reduced the government's tax revenue, leaving it with little money to spend on infrastructure projects.

Purchasing Managers Index

While GDP is a key quarterly economic indicator in all countries, the data aren't usually released until two or three months after the quarter has ended. That's a disadvantage for investors who need an immediate sense of how the economy is faring.

Investors, therefore, rely on a more up-to-date figure for insight into how an economy is performing. In many countries, it's called the Purchasing Managers Index, also known as the PMI.

The Central Statistics Office of Commonland surveys purchasing managers—the people in charge of buying goods and services for corporations—about business conditions. The office then compiles and publishes a monthly index that shows businesses' confidence for services and manufacturing. This forward-looking **leading indicator** is simple to understand. It shows business confidence.

A reading above 50 signifies optimism or expansion. A reading below 50 signifies pessimism or contraction.

In the following example, the PMI for manufacturing in Commonland for April was 51.5.

The *Commonland Express* reporter compared the figure with historical PMI data and wrote the following story. Note that the headline includes a superlative ("Weakest Pace in Seven Months") and that the lead and third paragraphs offer context ("a sign that"; "The data indicate").

Commonland Manufacturing Grows at Weakest Pace in Seven Months

Manufacturing in Commonland declined to a seven-month low, a sign that falling interest rates and government tax cuts haven't yet spurred consumer demand.

The Purchasing Managers Index for manufacturing, released by the Central Statistics Office of Commonland, dropped to 51.5 in April. That was the lowest reading since September last year.

The data indicate that policy makers may have to do more to revive consumer demand in Businessworld's second-largest economy. The Reserve Bank of Commonland slashed its benchmark rate six times last year to a record-low 1 percent. In January, the government cut tax rates for individuals and companies to stimulate growth.

The Society of Commonland Automobile Manufacturers may cut its annual domestic passenger-car sales target as slowing consumer demand hurt sales at companies including Stellarcars Co., Zoya Rohil, a senior director for the group, said last month. Rustic Steel Co. reported that profit last quarter dropped by a fifth from a year earlier.

While the 51.5 reading was the weakest in seven months, any number above 50 signifies expansion.

Inflation

On June 12, Commonland's Central Statistics Office announced inflation data for May.

Here are some excerpts from the press release:

Consumer price index in May: 2.2 percent (MoM)
Price data collected from select towns and villages by the Field Operations
    Division of the statistics office.

The *Commonland Express* reporter prepared templates for inflation accelerating and slowing.

Scanning the press release, she noted:

- The 2.2 percent gain in the inflation rate in May was the highest in two years.
- The rate breached the central bank's 2 percent inflation target for the first time in five years.
- The rate was higher than economists' median forecasts of a 2 percent gain.

- Inflation had accelerated mainly because of a spurt in the prices of milk, vegetables and pork.
- The inflation number came as economic growth slowed to a one-year low last quarter.

After calling an economist for comment, she wrote the following:

Commonland Inflation Accelerates, Breaching Central Bank's Target

Commonland's inflation accelerated to a two-year high, breaching the central bank's target and giving it less room to lower interest rates and stimulate economic growth.

Consumer prices rose 2.2 percent in May compared with the previous month, the statistics office said in a statement today. The jump exceeded economists' median forecast of a 2 percent increase.

It's the first time in five years that inflation has crossed the central bank's 2 percent target, restricting central bank Governor Anne Misha's scope to cut interest rates and spur consumer demand. The economy grew at the weakest pace in a year in the three months through March. Policy makers slashed borrowing costs six times last year to a record-low 1 percent.

"With inflation rearing its head and growth weakening, there is only one option—leave rates where they are for the moment," said Emma Garcia, an economist at Savings Co. in Fund City, Bankland. Garcia said she expected growth to keep slowing until the end of the year.

PRO TIP

How to measure inflation:

The most commonly used indicator to measure inflation is the Consumer Price Index, or CPI. To gauge how much prices are moving, the statistics office creates a basket of goods and services that people generally buy and tracks how the price of each item shifts over time.

Let's say it costs C$100 to buy the goods in the CPI basket in February, the month that the basket was created. In March, a month later, it costs C$102. The month-on-month increase is 2%, which is the CPI reading. The following February, the basket costs C$105. That's a 5% year-on-year change.

Another indicator that shows inflation is the GDP deflator. This shows the aggregate level of price increases by measuring the difference between real GDP and nominal GDP.

Style:

- As with GDP, journalists look at the percentage change in the inflation rate.

- Inflation is a rate of change in prices. Therefore, inflation may accelerate or slow.

- The inflation rate may rise or fall.

- Consumer prices may rise at a faster or slower pace.

- Writing "rising inflation" or "higher inflation" is redundant.

- Faster, or quicker, inflation is accurate.

YOUR TURN 4.3 Read the following report and complete the exercises below.

A report from the Foodland National Statistics Office

Introduction

Consumer price inflation is the rate at which the prices of goods and services bought by households rise or fall. Imagine a very large "shopping basket" containing goods and services commonly bought by families. As the prices of the items in the basket change over time, so does the total cost of the basket. Movements in indexes that track consumer prices represent the changing cost of the shopping basket.

Consumer price indexes are calculated by collecting a sample of prices for a selection of representative goods and services in a range of Foodland retail locations, including the internet. The contents of the basket of goods and services are updated annually to ensure the indexes reflect the most up-to-date trends in spending patterns.

Changes to the CPI "shopping basket"

Like most years, technological developments influence how the basket is updated. This year, we've added a smart speaker, such as Robo Corp.'s SpeakOut or Phonz Inc.'s Listenup. This type of equipment wasn't covered previously. We've also introduced a number of new items to represent specific markets where consumer spending is significant or growing. For example, we added bakeware to reflect increased expenditure in recent years, possibly influenced by the success of television cookery programs.

Similarly, flavored teas have been introduced due to their increased popularity shown by the shelf-space devoted to them in Foodland stores.

In addition, some items have been added to diversify the range of products collected for established groupings. Peanut butter has been introduced to improve coverage of oils and fats. Previously, margarine was the only item in the relevant subclass. Similarly, an electric toothbrush has been added to improve representation of electrical appliances in the personal care class. Popcorn bought in movie theaters is already included in the catering services part of the baskets but a new item has been added for popcorn sold in Foodland shops.

Some new items are direct replacements for similar products to reflect a change in buying habits. In furniture, settees have replaced three-piece suites. Dinner plates have replaced crockery sets. Dog treats have been added in place of dry dog food. Likewise, liquid laundry detergent has replaced the powdered variety.

Envelopes have also been removed from the miscellaneous printed matter and stationery part of the baskets, reflecting the increasing use of new technology for communication.

The proportion of household expenditure devoted to services has broadly risen over the last 25 years. This is reflected in an increasing weight for this component in the consumer price indexes and the addition of new items in the basket to improve measurement of price changes in this area: examples include fees for playgroups and carers who look after infants, the disabled, senior citizens and others.

Exercise 1:
Write a **headline, lead and second paragraph** for a breaking news story about changes in the "shopping basket" of items used in compiling consumer price inflation in Foodland.

Exercise 2:
Discuss **additional reporting** and possible **visual elements** that could be created for a 45-second TV item. What's the angle? Who would you speak to? What information would you put in a **social media post** to grab viewership?

Exercise 3:
Discuss additional reporting that would be needed for a **one-page magazine feature story** that will be published in two days. What's the angle? What's the headline on the story?

A week after the inflation announcement, the Reserve Bank of Commonland's Monetary Policy Committee met to decide on policy.

After the meeting, the central bank published the following press release:

Statement by Governor Anne Misha:

The Monetary Policy Committee deliberated extensively on current macroeconomic conditions and the outlook. Based on its assessment, the MPC voted to keep the policy rate unchanged. The committee, however, decided to persist with the accommodative stance as long as it is necessary to revive growth, while ensuring that inflation remains within the target.

The MPC noted that since its last meeting, Businessworld economic activity has remained subdued, though some signs of resilience are becoming visible.

Turning to domestic developments, real GDP growth moderated to 0.4 percent year-on-year in the three months through March, which is the weakest expansion in one year. Growth in automobiles and housing contracted but banking gained.

Consumer price inflation increased to 2.2 percent in May from April because of a surge in prices of milk, vegetables and port. That was higher than our set target of 2 percent.

The MPC revised the CPI inflation projection upward to 3 percent by September from 2 percent forecast earlier. It revised downward real GDP growth for the year through September to 1 percent from 1.5 percent.

As a consequence, the MPC unanimously judged that there is monetary policy space for future action but felt it appropriate for a pause at this juncture and to maintain the benchmark interest rate at 1 percent.

Within minutes of the press release, Commonland's main stock index fell 1.2 percent, the most in three weeks. The Commonland dollar strengthened 0.1 percent to C$2.30 per Energyland dollar.

The index fell because seven of nine economists surveyed by the *Commonland Express* had expected the central bank to cut its policy rate by a quarter point. The other two had forecast no change.

The *Commonland Express*'s reporter wrote this story:

Commonland Central Bank Resists Rate-Cut Pressure as Inflation Spikes

The Reserve Bank of Commonland defied expectations for an interest rate cut after inflation breached the central bank's target.

Policy makers in Businessworld's second-largest economy unanimously voted to keep the benchmark rate at a record-low 1 percent, according to a statement. Seven of nine analysts surveyed by the *Commonland Express* predicted a quarter-point cut. Two estimated no change.

The surprise move shows central bank Governor Anne Misha has shifted her strategy on inflation after it quickened to a two-year high in May. The unexpected decision sent the stock index down by the most in three weeks, while the Commonland dollar strengthened against the Energyland dollar. The central bank can afford to pause after it delivered six rate cuts last year to spur consumer demand.

"Governor Misha has shown her true colors here—as an inflation fighter," said Pankaj Castro, an economist at Peak Analytics Co. in Diversia. Castro had forecast a quarter-point cut.

The central bank raised its inflation projection to 3 percent by September from 2 percent earlier. It cut its year-on-year economic growth forecast to 1 percent from 1.5 percent.

Fiscal Policy

It's July 1 in Commonland, and Finance Minister Sunita Tej is preparing to read out her budget proposals in parliament for the financial year, or fiscal year, starting on Oct. 1. In some non-parliamentary countries, the president submits a budget proposal to the elected political body, such as Congress, that is in charge of spending and borrowing.

Note that the **fiscal year** begins on different dates in different countries. In some nations, the fiscal year and the calendar year are the same.

The **budget** lays out the government's spending and revenue-generation projections for the year. It also estimates the government's total expenses and income.

For the past two years, Commonland has posted a **budget deficit**, meaning government expenses have exceeded income. That happened as the slowing economy hurt company profit, thereby reducing tax revenues. Until two years ago, Commonland had a **budget surplus** in most years.

Finance Minister Tej and her advisers deliberated about how to fund the budget shortfall. One option was for the government to sell bonds to commercial banks. Another was to raise taxes, although this was politically unpopular and could affect consumer demand. A third option was for the government to sell stakes in some state-run companies.

In her budget speech, Tej said her priority was to spur consumer demand and boost economic growth.

Budget highlights included:

- A 30 percent increase in public-works spending. Construction of roads, railways and airports will spur demand for steel and cement, among other projects, and lead to more construction industry jobs.
- Tax incentives for home buyers. Tej said purchase of new houses would trigger demand for household products such as refrigerators, air conditioners and furniture.
- A cut in the personal income tax rate to 22 percent from 25 percent to boost the disposable income of households.
- A cut in the corporate tax rate to 38 percent from 40 percent to help encourage investment.
- New measures to temper climate change, including more subsidies for people opting for solar panels and home insulation.

As a result of the increased spending and other measures, Tej said, the budget deficit will widen to 3 percent of Commonland's GDP in the next fiscal year, from 2.1 percent in the previous year. She added that the government would sell bonds to bridge the gap.

Predictably, the financial markets reacted to Tej's speech:

- The stock index surged 4.4 percent, the biggest increase in 18 months, led by steel, automobile and construction companies. Stocks advanced on optimism that tax cuts and higher spending would boost economic expansion and spur company profit.

- The yield on Commonland's benchmark 10-year government bonds rose five basis points to 3.77 percent. Bond investors were concerned that the government's growing debt load might lead rating companies to cut the nation's credit rating.
- The Commonland dollar gained 0.6 percent to C$1.9 per Energyland dollar.

The *Commonland Express* reporter wrote this story:

Commonland Cuts Taxes, Boosts Spending to Revive Growth

Commonland's finance minister cut personal and corporate tax rates and increased public-works spending to boost consumer demand in Businessworld's second-largest economy.

The measures, announced as part of the government budget for the financial year starting on Oct. 1, are essential to jump-starting the economy, Sunita Tej said in a speech today. Growth slowed to a one-year low in the January-to-March quarter.

"The government has finally done something dramatic to prop up growth," said Pankaj Castro, an economist at Peak Analytics Co. in Diversia. "The last thing we want is stagflation—growth stagnating and the inflation rate climbing."

Tej said the measures will widen the budget deficit to 3 percent of gross domestic product in the next fiscal year starting Oct. 1 from 2.1 percent in the current year. She said the government will sell bonds to pay for the projects.

The stock index jumped the most in 18 months, and the Commonland dollar gained on optimism the measures will stimulate economic expansion. Commonland's 10-year government bonds fell, sending yields higher, on concern the nation's debt burden could jeopardize its credit rating.

Inflation accelerated to a two-year high in May, prompting the central bank to keep the key interest rate unchanged after reducing it six times last year to a record-low 1 percent. The economy grew 0.4 percent in the three months through March, the weakest pace in a year.

The *Commonland Express* published a box alongside the story including all the notable figures in the budget.

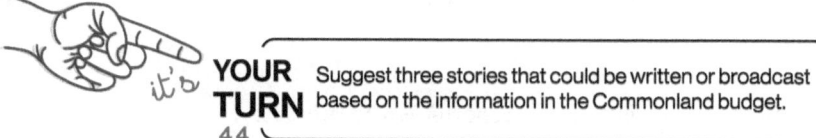

YOUR TURN 4.4 Suggest three stories that could be written or broadcast based on the information in the Commonland budget.

What other content is needed?

Who should be interviewed?

What key questions need to be asked?

How would you report and write these stories?

Government Bonds

Investors consider bonds to be a safe asset for their money because investors are assured of receiving a fixed coupon rate, which is a fixed return on their investment.

Stocks, on the other hand, are riskier. The price of a share could plummet—there is no guarantee of an ensured return.

Bonds are not free from risk. Companies and even governments sometimes fail to pay the interest and principal on their debt. But when a company goes bankrupt, bondholders typically stand a greater chance of getting back some of their money than shareholders do.

When an economy faces risks such as an economic slowdown or political instability, investors typically move their investments from risky assets to bonds. When that happens, stock prices fall and bond prices rise, pushing bond yields down.

Similarly, when the economy is in good shape, investors are usually willing to take more risks. As a result, stocks rise and bond prices fall, pushing up the yield.

PRO TIP

Three things to remember about government bonds:

1. The benchmark government bond is often the 10-year bond that's most traded. The benchmark changes frequently.
2. As with corporate bonds, the coupon rate and the maturity date are needed to identify a government bond.
3. Journalists normally focus on the yield, rather than the bond's price, to show how a bond has performed. For example, the yield on Commonland's 3.24% bond maturing in May 2031 rose five basis points to 6.24% today. Or, Commonland's benchmark 10-year notes yielded 6.24% at the close today. Bonds and notes mean the same thing. Bills or treasury bills are shorter duration bonds, typically with a maturity of less than one year.

Why Do Reporters Focus on Government Bond Yields?

Bond yields shed light on the state of the economy.

They reflect interest-rate expectations in the bond market, as well as inflation expectations and creditworthiness. When bond yields are rising, bond investors expect the central bank to raise the benchmark rate. Conversely, falling yields show that investors expect the central bank to cut this rate.

Yields can also be viewed as the interest rate that lenders such as institutional investors are demanding from governments that want to borrow money. The more risky the government, the higher the interest rate that borrowers would demand to buy the bond.

How Are Government Bonds Sold?

Government bonds are sold in **auctions** (figure 4.1). These auctions are conducted by central banks on behalf of their governments. In some

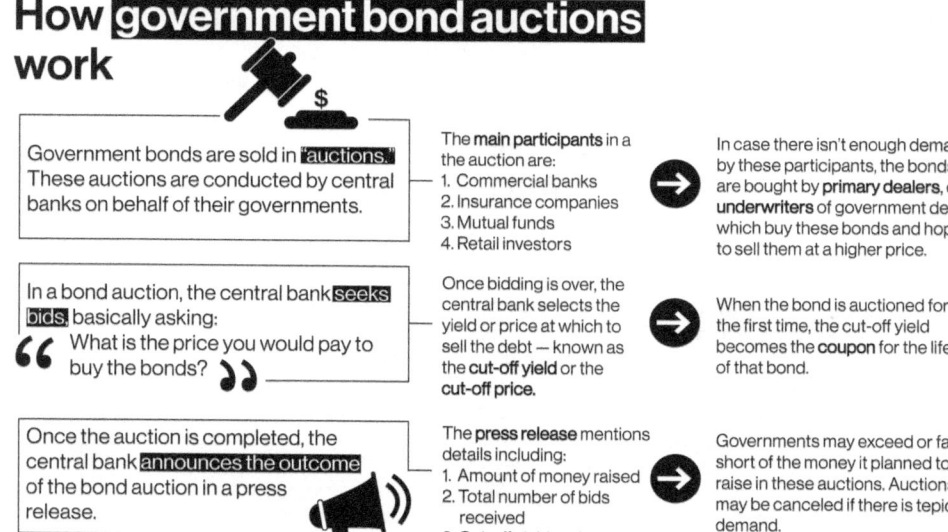

FIGURE 4.1 How government bonds are sold.

countries, bond sales are managed by debt offices. The main participants in a government-bond auction are commercial banks, insurance companies, mutual funds and retail investors.

Note, in some countries, bond auctions may take place only via primary dealers. For more on bonds, see chapter 3.

Currencies

A currency is money used in exchange for goods and services. It is typically issued by a government and circulates in a country's economy. A currency's value against other currencies depends on supply and demand. In the past decade, digital currencies have emerged as alternatives to government-backed currencies.

Journalists reporting on any country's economy need to understand how currency exchange rates work. Since all countries trade and invest in others, it's important to know whether the currency in one country is strengthening or weakening against those elsewhere.

The exchange rate is a barometer of an economy's performance and well-being because it shows investors' perceptions about a country. When foreign investors buy stocks, bonds, commodities or other assets in a country, the currency strengthens. When they pull their investments out, the currency weakens.

All currencies are quoted in pairs, normally with the dominant currency in the world. For example, the Commonland dollar, like all the currencies in Businessworld, is benchmarked against the Energyland dollar, which is Businessworld's **reserve currency** (figure 4.2)

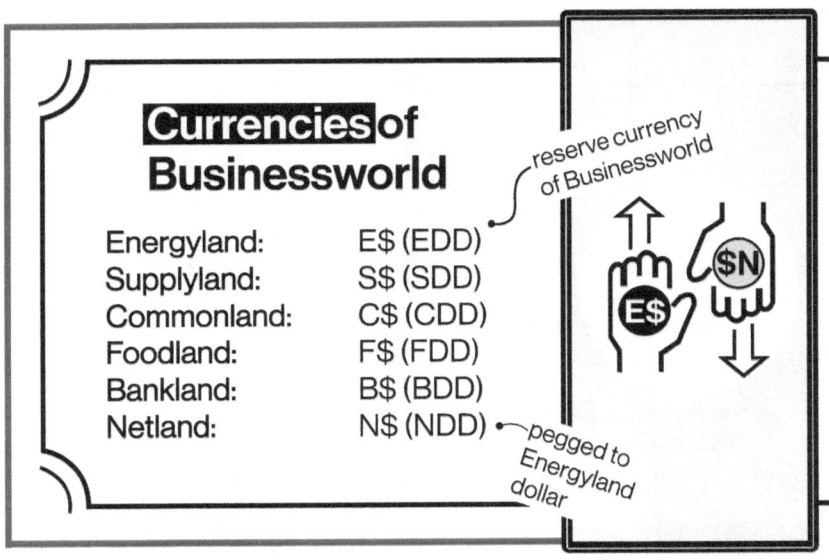

FIGURE 4.2 The currencies of Businessworld.

In other words, other countries hold the Energyland dollar in reserve so that it can be used to make international payments for goods and services.

A typical **foreign-exchange** (also known as **forex**) story would explain how much the currency has moved against the Energyland dollar today, and why. But business journalists should add paragraphs about specific currencies in other stories when appropriate. For example, currency fluctuations can have a significant impact on a company's bottom line if it generates a large percentage of revenue overseas and repatriates its profits.

Here's how one reporter added a currency paragraph in an earnings story about Stellarcars Co., a Commonland automaker:

> Some of Stellarcars' earnings gain can be attributed to a decline in the Commonland dollar, the worst-performing major currency against the Energyland dollar in the past six months. The slump is a boon for the Commonland automaker because it increases the value of its repatriated profit.

What does it mean when a currency strengthens or weakens?

Currencies are priced relative to each other and are quoted in pairs. When talking about a currency strengthening or weakening, the assumption is that it's being compared to the reserve currency. To be totally clear, it's best to specify.

All currencies have a three-letter code. The Energyland dollar's is **EDD**. The Commonland dollar's is **CDD**. The codes are used to pair a currency and show the value of the exchange rate.

Commandland's currency is paired this way: EDDCDD. The Energyland dollar is the base currency and the Commonland dollar is the quoted currency.

For example, EDDCDD = 2 means that one Energyland dollar could be exchanged for two Commonland dollars. But if EDDCDD = 2.02, it would mean that one Energyland dollar could buy 2.02 Commonland dollars. In other words, the Commonland dollar has weakened against the Energyland dollar.

Assume a year from now, EDDCDD = 1.8. This means you would get fewer Commonland dollars — 1.8 — for every Energyland dollar. So the Commonland dollar has strengthened against the Energyland dollar.

Other Economic Indicators

As well as GDP, inflation and the Purchasing Managers Index, business journalists look at numerous other economic indicators for clues about how an economy is performing.

Among the most important are data on unemployment and jobs creation, trade in goods and services, retail sales, homebuilding and house prices, industrial production and consumer confidence.

Jobs

There are strong correlations between unemployment, jobs creation and GDP. Economies tend to shrink when people lose their jobs because unemployed people cut their spending. Conversely, economies tend to boom when jobs are created.

Here's the first four paragraphs of a story published on the *Commonland Express*'s website after the release of jobless data. Note how the lead contains a superlative—"first time in three years"—and it explains to the reader what the news means. The actual numbers are given in the fourth paragraph:

Jobless Claims in Commonland Top 100,000 for First Time in Three Years

> The number of Commonland citizens applying for unemployment benefits rose above 100,000 for the first time in three years, suggesting the economic slump is deepening in Businessworld's second-largest economy.
>
> The bigger-than-expected rise in claims underlines the difficulties that Commonland Prime Minister Greg Ravi and the central bank face to generate jobs while keeping inflation under control.
>
> "The government's planned tax cuts and increased public-works spending are two good steps on the road to recovery," said Pankaj Castro, an economist at Peak Analytics Co. in Diversia. "But I fear it's a long road. The government will need to take bolder actions before the end of the year."

Initial jobless claims rose by 18,798 to 103,963 in the week ended July 5, Labor Department data showed Thursday. Economists were expecting initial claims of 97,543 on the basis of median estimates.

Trade

Besides covering surprises in routine trade data—an unexpected jump in imports, perhaps, or a rise in the deficit—journalists reporting on a nation's economy need to monitor trade relations between countries. Sometimes these go awry, resulting in skirmishes or a more ominous trade war.

Trade wars are often sparked by one nation's perception that another is engaging in unfair trading practices, such as deliberately keeping its currency weak to boost exports. One frequent outcome is **protectionism**—when a country protects its domestic industries by restricting imports via tariffs, quotas and other rules.

In economies dependent on overseas sales of goods and services, the value and variety of **exports** is a key indicator. In other economies, **import** data may signal economic imbalances. When a wheat-exporting nation suddenly begins to import the grain, for example, it's worth finding out why.

There's no right or wrong way to write a trade story. Many focus on the latest data. Others may lead on a specific data set, such as a sudden increase in defense sales from one country to another. Yet others may examine a trend in trade such as the reasons for a prolonged decline in trade to a region, or they may analyze forthcoming trade talks for hints of a breakthrough.

Here are the first four paragraphs of a typical trade story that is based on just-released data:

Commonland Trade Gap Narrows as Steel Spurs Record Export Jump

Commonland's trade deficit narrowed in June for the first time in nine months as a surge in demand for steel from Foodland and Netland spurred exports.

The nation's exports are also benefiting from a recent decline in the value of the Commonland dollar, which makes the country's goods more competitive in foreign markets. Automobile and cement shipments also rose.

The overall gap in trade of goods and services narrowed to C$50.6 billion from C$52 billion a month earlier, according to data released by the Central Statistics Office in Diversia. That compared with the median estimate of C$51.9 billion in a *Commonland Express* survey of 17 economists.

Exports increased by a record 9.6 percent to C$158.3 billion from the previous month. Imports climbed 4.7 percent to C$208.9 billion.

Housing

Residential housing statistics are among the most closely watched economic indicators. These include **housing starts**—the number of new buildings being constructed—as well as sales of new or previously owned homes, house price changes, building permits and mortgage applications.

Any surge in home construction shows that consumers are confident about the economy, willing to assume a multiyear mortgage and ready to spend on everything from carpets and couches to televisions, paint and garden accessories.

Here are examples of story headlines generated by following housing data:

Commonland Existing-Home Sales Surged in July by Most on Record

Suburban-Home Prices Gain as City Dwellers Venture Out of Town

Copper, Nickel Rise Amid Increased Demand for New Netland Homes

Netland Economic Rebound Picks Up Speed on Home, Car Sales

Gnomes, Greenhouses in Vogue at Garden Centers as Housing Booms

Retail Sales, Industrial Production

Most countries issue monthly retail sales and industrial production data. Investors and economists track retail sales to gauge consumer demand for products at stores and via the internet.

They examine industrial production statistics to see how well the manufacturing, mining and utilities sectors are performing. An increase in industrial production may signal higher consumption at home and a rise in exports.

After retail sales and industrial production data were released on the same day in Commonland, the *Commonland Express*'s economy reporter wrote the following:

Commonland Retail Sales, Industrial-Output Grow Slower than Expected

> Retail sales and industrial production rose at a slower pace than expected in July, underscoring a moderation in the economy's rebound.
>
> The value of retail purchases increased 1.2 percent from June, according to Central Statistics Office data released Friday. A separate report showed total output at factories, mines and utilities rose 3 percent in July from the prior month.
>
> Retail sales were pulled down by a decline in purchases of cars and home furnishings, as well as weaker-than-estimated gains at restaurants and clothing stores. Online sales rose for a 17th successive month. Commonland's stock index fell 0.5 percent after the reports. Government bonds rose and the Commonland dollar weakened.
>
> "These are worrying signals," Pankaj Castro, an economist at Peak Analytics Co. in Diversia, said on CTV. "The rate cuts so far have failed to kick-start demand."
>
> Economists surveyed by the *Commonland Express* had forecast a 1.5 percent increase in retail sales in July and a 4.2 percent gain in industrial production.

Consumer Confidence

As noted earlier, business confidence data such as the Purchasing Managers Index help corporate leaders make decisions about investment, employment and sales in the months ahead. They use consumer confidence data in a similar way.

To determine consumers' confidence, governments and other organizations survey individual consumers about their attitudes now and expectations for the future, known as **consumer sentiment**. The index they produce is based on factors such as consumers' willingness to buy durable goods, their income growth and savings, and their perceived job security.

Here's how the *Commonwealth Express* began one such story:

Commonland Consumer Confidence Slumps to Six-Year Low on Jobs, Pay

Commonland citizens are less confident about their financial well-being and the economic outlook than at any time in the past six years, a government report shows.

The monthly consumer confidence index report for August points to a bumpy economic recovery—and risks for Prime Minister Greg Ravi's reelection—as residents grapple with rising unemployment, low income growth and uncertainty about the government's stimulus plans.

"This report should be a wake-up call for the government because it reveals consumers' deep dissatisfaction with their own living conditions and with Ravi's economic policies," Braini Inclicki, a fund manager at Gasopolis Asset Management Co. in Energyland, said in a phone interview.

The index, a composite measure of financial health and economic expectations, slid to 38.8 from 41.7 in July and from 48 a year ago, the report said. The median estimate of nine economists surveyed by the *Commonland Express* called for a reading of 39. A number below 50 suggests consumers' views are net negative.

Legislation

Virtually all government legislation—whether it's a move to approve a drug for sale, to change e-commerce guidelines or to regulate social media—affects business in some way.

It's the business reporters' job to explain to their audience the likely **financial consequences** of the legislation as well as the potential opportunities and challenges. Because most government activity involves money—usually spending it or saving it—there are winners and losers for every proposed law.

YOUR TURN 4.5 Your government is proposing "No Fly" legislation to stop airlines taking off or landing between 11 p.m. and 6 a.m. At present, the rules state no activity between midnight and 5 a.m. Consider the likely impact on airlines and airports and their employees, individuals who live near airports, schools, hotels, parking lots, restaurants, environmentalists and others.

Who are the winners and losers, and how?

What's the potential monetary impact?

Write three 12-word headlines and explain how you would go about covering each story.

Politics and the Economy

Politics affects every citizen's life and livelihood, so it's imperative that business journalists keep track of who's in power, who's up-and-coming and, above all, why politicians are promoting certain policies.

Money is involved in virtually every decision. And as we've noted before, it's the reporter's job to **follow the money**.

That means tracking donations to political parties and individuals as well as examining corporate lobbying and event sponsorships. It means questioning, for example, why one district in a country has better roads and bridges than another or why the police are better funded in one city than elsewhere. The phrase "All politics is local" refers in part to the belief that political events at the local level help shape national and even international economic policies.

When writing political stories, whether about an individual politician or an election campaign, always consider the economic and market impact of the event. Let's look, for example, at how an election campaign played out in Commonland and how the *Commonland Express* reporter handled it.

Politics in Action

Prime Minister Greg Ravi's tenure is ending, and he is seeking a second term in this parliamentary democracy.

Ravi is campaigning on the promise that his Commonland Progressive Party will revive the economy and create jobs. At every rally, he lists steps that his government has taken to rekindle consumer demand and to fight inflation.

In contrast, the main opposition party, the Commonland Liberal Democratic Alliance, is plagued by infighting and lack of a cohesive plan to defeat the incumbent.

Ravi wins by a landslide, prompting dramatic movements in Commonland's financial markets.

The *Commonland Express*'s reporter wrote the short story below for the website, shortly after the result was confirmed.

Points to note:

- The story was written for a national, rather than an international, audience.
- The headline has more than one element, noting what the victory means for the nation's currency.
- "strongest performance in a quarter century" and "biggest increase in six months" are useful superlatives for context.

Ravi Wins Landslide Election Victory in Commonland; Dollar Soars
Prime Minister Greg Ravi won a decisive majority in Commonland's general election as voters were attracted to his promises to create jobs and control inflation.

Ravi's Commonland Progressive Party enjoyed its strongest performance in a quarter century, winning 302 seats in the 545-member parliament. In the run-up to the election, Ravi's government cut personal and corporate taxes and increased spending on roads and bridges.

The Commonland dollar gained the most in two years, strengthening 0.8 percent to E$1.30. The stock index gained 3.8 percent, the biggest increase in six months. Benchmark 10-year bonds fell, pushing the yield up three basis points to 3.07 percent.

The Final Word

Economic data are the staples of most country stories. These leading and lagging indicators provide instantaneous market-moving news of the highest value. Equally important for readers is the analysis of what these economic statistics mean for the country, companies, policy, politics and the markets.

The most enterprising reporters and writers go one step further. They keep an eye on so-called proxy indicators—such as data on power consumption or even the sale of toothpaste and shampoo in certain areas—to gain perspective on the strength of consumer demand.

The best way to tell the country story is through the words and actions of the people who live, play and work there. These human anecdotes breathe life into any country story, illuminating society's challenges and opportunities, strengths and weaknesses.

5

• • • •

The Commodities Story

The First Word

A commodity is a product that is either **grown**, like corn and wheat, or **extracted** from the earth, like coal, oil and gold.

Commodities are the most tangible and visible of all the financial assets. Wheat, rice, coffee, cocoa and other agricultural products are dietary staples. Oil and gas heat homes and fuel cars. Lithium and other rare-earth metals power smartphones. Precious metals such as gold, silver, platinum and palladium are used in everything from catalytic converters and computer chips to dental equipment and designer jewelry.

Long before trading in stocks, bonds and currencies became popular, agricultural produce was bought and sold using **futures contracts**, or agreements to sell goods at a later date. (For more on futures contracts, see chapter 6.) Today, business journalists focus on commodities that are grown or raised, known as **soft commodities**, and on products that are mined or extracted, called **hard commodities**.

This chapter examines commodities from the perspective of sugarcane grown in Foodland, metals mined in Commonland and oil produced in Energyland.

You will learn the following in this chapter:

- Why the commodities beat is so attractive to business journalists
- How to cover commodities—from agriculture and precious metals to oil and gas
- How to write commodities stories

Reporting on Commodities

Commodities make the world go round. Since ancient times, commodities have linked places of production with places of commerce and consumption. At one time, camels, horse-drawn wagons and water-borne vessels helped transport the most precious commodities, such as salt, silk and spices, along well-worn trade routes. These days, tankers, bulk carriers, container ships and railroads transport the commodities that are most in demand—oil, gas, grain, ore and other metals and foodstuffs.

At its best, commodities reporting demands broad and deep knowledge of how and why the prices of crops and raw materials move. It requires the journalist to follow the story from the point of production on a farm or in a mine along the supply chain to the end user, the consumer (figure 5.1).

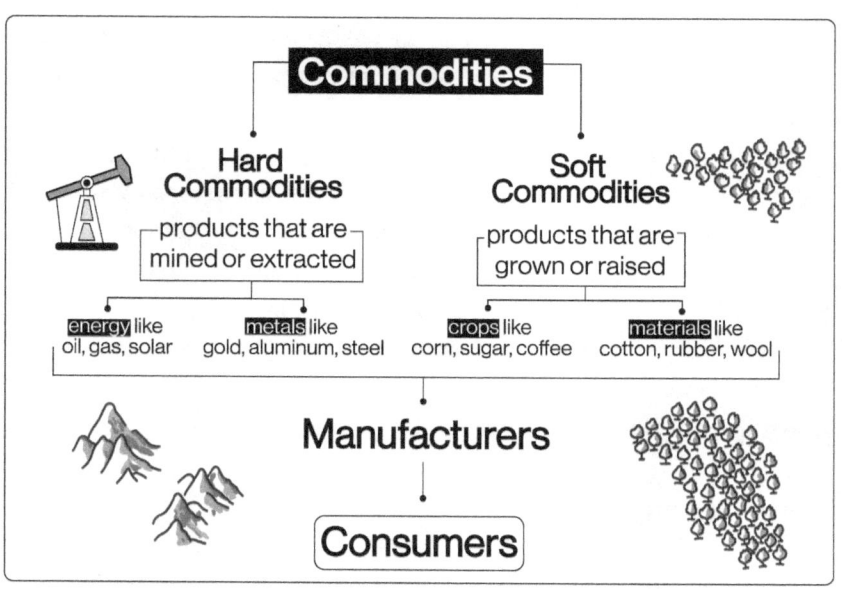

FIGURE 5.1 Different types of commodities.

When savvy commodities reporters join the dots, local stories become more global and have more impact. A story about rising corn prices, for example, could include context about the companies that use the commodity in their breakfast-cereal products. A story about oil prices sinking could examine whether the cost of gasoline has also fallen or whether energy-company profit margins have widened.

Unexpected incidents—a war, a forest fire, a flood, a workers' strike, a shipwreck, a power failure, an act of terrorism, to name a few—have immediate implications for the prices and movement of commodities.

So, too, do more mundane events—the signing of a trade pact, regulatory or policy changes, inventory reports from government and non-governmental agencies and industry groups, and extreme weather caused by climate change.

The commodities reporter must be agile and ready to **identify what's driving the price changes**, what's at stake and what the repercussions will be for businesses, governments and consumers.

PRO TIP

Most commodity stories cite the **futures price** — the price at which the buyer will receive a certain quantity of the raw material on an agreed-upon date. For example, the benchmark price of coffee is based on a blend that will be delivered one or two months in the future. In late January, investors and speculators will buy and sell the March contract.

By contrast, when reporting on precious metals such as gold, silver, platinum and palladium, use the **spot price** — the price at which the commodity is trading right now, in real time. The decision on whether to cite the spot or the futures price depends on the commodity and the circumstances.

The Crops Crisis

Agriculture is the mainstay of Foodland's economy and its biggest employer. About 60 percent of the country's gross domestic product derives from locally manufactured foodstuffs.

Sugar is Foodland's main crop and biggest export. Its omnipresence helped spawn several companies including Sip Corp., the energy-drinks maker, and Sweeti Inc., the confectioner.

A sugarcane crop requires thousands of liters of water to produce a kilo of the commodity. Foodland's rainy season, from June to September, usually produces adequate water supplies to fill the nation's reservoirs. But by late July one year, agricultural experts in Foodland became concerned that the country was experiencing its driest summer in a decade. Sugar and other crops were suffering. The economy suddenly appeared vulnerable.

Late on July 25, Finance Minister Bella Manek called a surprise press conference. Reporters rushed to the ministry in anticipation of a major announcement.

Foodland was facing its worst drought in at least 20 years, hitting the quantity and quality of its sugar harvest, Manek said. That was reducing exports and could force the country to import essential items such as rice, milk and corn, she added.

Manek's comments had an immediate impact on the cost of sugar contracts traded in Businessworld. And when trading began at the Commodity Exchange of Energyland on July 26, sugar futures for October jumped 16 percent to a record 13.45 Energyland cents per pound.

It was a major story throughout Businessworld because Foodland was the biggest sugar supplier.

One website headline said:

Sugar Price Leaps 16 Percent as Foodland Drought Curtails Exports

The *Foodland Times*'s story began:

Sugar Jumps 16 Percent as Drought Harms Harvest, Dries Up Supplies

Sugar prices jumped 16 percent to a record today as the worst drought in 20 years reduced supplies available for export from Foodland.

The crisis, highlighted last night by Finance Minister Bella Manek, threatens to harm Foodland's economy because agriculture is the biggest contributor to the nation's gross domestic product and its biggest employer.

White-sugar futures for delivery in October soared to 13.45 Energyland cents a pound from 11.60.

Later that day, Sip Corp. posted on the social-media platform Squeaker that the disruption in sugar supplies was forcing the company to cut production. As a result, it would temporarily close one factory that employs 250 people. Sweeti Inc. followed, saying that it would temporarily lay off 100 people at one of its Foodland processing plants.

The *Foodland Times* updated the story on its website with the impact on companies and the economy, plus a comment from an analyst:

Sip Shuts Plant, Sweeti Cuts Jobs as Foodland Drought Hits Sugar Supplies

Sip Corp. plans to shut a factory and Sweeti Inc. said it will cut workers as the worst drought in Foodland in 20 years hurts sugar exports from Businessworld's largest supplier.

Sugar jumped 16 percent to a record 13.45 Energyland cents a pound after Finance Minister Bella Manek said the drought was affecting the quality and quantity of sugar. Sugar exports will fall substantially, she said.

As sugar production shrinks, other companies may be forced to close factories, at least temporarily, economists and employers said. That would mean higher prices for sugar and all the food products that use the sweetener, according to Michelle Chua, a market strategist at Toe Stock Broking Co. in Teaville.

"We are still some distance away from prices peaking," Chua said. "The knock-on effect of the drought could have severe consequences for the Foodland economy."

YOUR TURN 5.1 Let's turn our focus to wheat in Energyland. Write a headline and a two-paragraph story using the following information:

On Friday, Feb. 28, wheat futures for April in Energyland rose 0.4% to E$5.60 a bushel. This was the highest close since Aug. 31.

Analysts said prices of winter wheat varieties were rising because heavy snow had harmed the crop and prevented farmers from transporting it to Energyland ports for export.

Traders said they expected stockpiles of the commodity to decline this year. They also noted that Energyland's Department of Agriculture was set to release monthly supply and demand estimates for wheat, soybeans, corn and other agricultural commodities later on Friday.

The Miners' Strike

Commonland is Businessworld's biggest exporter of steel and home to some of the biggest producers, including GiantSteel Corp. and Rustic Steel Co.

Most workers at these companies are members of a powerful trade union, the Steel Workers' Union of Commonland, which has been demanding a wage increase of 4 percent a year. The management has refused to budge. Almost half the workers went on strike in early December.

At noon on Feb. 28, the Central Statistics Office of Commonland released data for industrial production for December. The statistics showed that steel production fell by 34 percent in December from a year earlier, the biggest drop in six years. Production, also known as output, was 14 percent lower than in November, the statistics office said.

Here's how the commodities reporter at the *Commonland Express* covered the story as soon as the numbers were released. Note that the reporter wrote in a bullet-point format as a way to get the story out quickly.

Commonland Steel Production Plunges Most in Six Years on Worker Strike

Steel output in Commonland dropped the most in six years after a strike at the nation's two largest steelmakers hampered production.

- Production fell 34 percent in December from a year earlier and was 14 percent lower than in November, the Central Statistics Office said in a statement on its website.

Key Insights

- The strike, now in its 85th day, shows no sign of ending. Managers at GiantSteel Corp. and Rustic Steel Co. broke off talks with the Steel Workers' Union earlier this month.
- The production cuts will probably reduce Commonland GDP by 0.5 percent this year if the strike lasts through the first quarter, economists say.
- Steel exports from Commonland fell to a four-year low in January, according to government data.

Market Reaction

- GiantSteel shares fell 1 percent and Rustic declined 0.8 percent. GiantSteel has dropped 11 percent and Rustic 8 percent since the strike began.

Bad News for Bankland

Shares of Bankland-based Build Co. plunged on the news from Commonland. The stock fell 8 percent, the biggest drop in nine years. Why would it decline?

Some context: Bankland is in the midst of an economic slowdown. To counter the deceleration, the government a year ago stepped up spending on roads, bridges and airports.

Build Co. won the bulk of the contracts for the government's public-works program. The company's stock surged 72 percent last year on optimism that it would post higher sales and profits.

The workers' strike in Commonland is particularly bad news for Build because Bankland depends on Commonland for most of its steel.

As steel exports from Commonland fell and with no end to the strike in sight, some of Build's construction projects had to be delayed.

A local website in Bankland ran several stories. These were the headlines:

Bankland Airport Project at Standstill Owing to Commonland Steel Strike

Build Shares Plunge as Strike in Commonland Stalls Steel Imports

Airport Construction Workers Laid Off as Commonland Strike Bites

Bankland Opposition Parties Call on Government to Find New Steel Sources

How Bankland Is a Hostage to Commonland Steel Fiasco: Analysis

YOUR TURN 5.2

In the Bankland example above, the local website touched on several angles. The editor asked the reporter for some graphics or other visual ideas to illustrate the stories.

Write three paragraphs suggesting specific visual images that the website could use. Each paragraph should contain a different theme.

Finite Resources

Elsewhere in Businessworld, there are other challenges. Energyland is Businessworld's richest nation and the biggest producer and exporter of oil. Oil accounts for 70 percent of gross domestic product. For the past 50 years, the country has relied on oil exports to propel its economy.

It now faces a problem. The global climate is changing, Energyland's oil resources are diminishing, and countries such as Supplyland and Bankland have taken the lead in switching to renewable energies such as wind and solar power. Meanwhile, Netland has become the world's biggest maker of electric cars, and Foodland has started to plant 400 million trees to offset carbon emissions.

Energyland's prime minister, Khalil Smithe, is under pressure to announce realistic solutions to the country's oil dilemma. The main issues are how to sustain economic growth and to create jobs as Businessworld weans itself off oil.

On March 3, after months of preparation, Prime Minister Smithe called a media conference to announce his plans for Energyland's future.

Here's what he said:

"Oil will play a dominant role in Energyland for the foreseeable future, but the reality is that oil won't be there forever. I want Energyland to become a global hub for banking and finance and to provide back-office software support to industries throughout Businessworld."

This will require "a lot of training of the country's youth and will mean that local universities will need to tie up with counterparts abroad," Smithe said.

Smithe said the government was in talks with investors, banks and insurance companies to invite them to set up branches in Energyland. To entice them, he said the government will offer 10-year tax breaks and subsidized office rents. Lastly, he said, Energyland was considering building a Businessworld theme park to attract more visitors from its neighbors.

The goal, Smithe said, was for the share of oil in the economy to drop to 30 percent in 20 years and for the services industry to drive Energyland growth.

The *Commonland Express* reporter asked her editor what she thought the main story was and how the website should handle the story. They decided to focus on the shift to banking and software. They also decided to write short sidebar stories about

- The suggested tax breaks
- The training challenges
- University tie-ups
- Energyland's tourism potential

Here's how the *Commonland Express* handled the main story. Note how the lead is specific about what Energyland is doing, and why. The third paragraph is a short, pithy quote, and the fourth paragraph, beginning "The overhaul marks," adds context about what the news means:

Energyland to Shift Focus to Banking, Software as Oil Runs Out

Energyland will try to entice banks and software companies with 10-year tax breaks and subsidized offices as part of a plan to steer its economy through oil's waning dominance.

The country wants services, including finance and back-office software support, to take over as the biggest contributor to gross domestic product within two decades, Prime Minister Khalil Smithe told reporters today. His government has been under pressure from opposition politicians and environmental groups to announce concrete plans to shift toward renewable energy.

"The reality is that oil won't be there forever, and we need to take bold steps to be ready," Smithe said.

The overhaul marks a major shift in policy for Businessworld's biggest energy producer. Until now, Energyland has largely ignored a push by neighboring countries to cleaner energy. Supplyland and Bankland already generate 50 percent of their energy from wind, solar and biomass, while Netland has become Businessworld's biggest maker of electric cars.

Foodland, meanwhile, has said it will plant 400 million trees as a way to offset carbon and methane emissions from its 80 million cows.

Smithe's plan envisions reducing crude's share in Energyland's GDP to 30 percent in 20 years from 70 percent now. To achieve this, it will build a hub for banking and finance in the capital, Gasopolis, Smithe said. Other initiatives outlined today include construction of a theme park designed to attract visitors from throughout Businessworld.

YOUR TURN 5.3 A *Commonland Express* reporter interviews Prime Minister Greg Ravi for an update on the country's plans to export oil. She writes a short story and the markets react to the news. Below is an updated story from the reporter. It needs editing. Rewrite the headline and write a three-paragraph story.

Pureoil, Commonland Refinery Oil Exports Face Delay on Infrastructure

The output of crude oil deposits being developed by Commonland companies such as Pureoil Co. and Commonland Refinery Corp. is unlikely to be exported soon because of the scale of the infrastructure projects required to transport the commodity out of the country, Prime Minister Gret Ravi said in an interview. Shares of Pureoil and Commonland Refinery, the nation's two largest oil companies, dropped 1.9% and 2.1% respectively, while the Commonland dollar declines 0.8% per Energyland dollar following the exclusive interview.

The government of Commonland, where oil was discovered a decade ago, said last year it expected to begin shipping crude within four years. "That timetable will probably need to be adjusted again," Ravi said today, because numerous challenges must be overcome, including a lack of finance to build pipelines and other infrastructure projects. It may take another four years to start exports, Ravi said.

Commodities prices can also be influenced by broader events in financial markets. Some commodities are considered "haven" assets. At times of market turbulence, investors will typically switch from riskier assets such as stocks into assets that are perceived as more stable, such as gold or bonds.

Investors shift their portfolio to keep their money safe and to prevent any loss from the economic crisis. When investors switch to haven assets, they are essentially **hedging** their risks. **Safe haven** is a way to describe the best hedge for an asset during a crisis.

In the above case, gold could be considered a "strong hedge" because it is negatively correlated with stocks.

YOUR TURN 5.4

It's 5 p.m. Thursday, Feb. 23, in Energyland. Today, the price of gold fell 1.4% to E$1,949.53 per ounce. Your editor asks you to write a headline and a story of no more than four paragraphs about gold using the following information:

Today's drop was the fourth successive day of declines. Gold has fallen 7.59% so far this year.

Energyland will release jobs data for January at 8:30 a.m. tomorrow, Feb. 24. In December, the unemployment rate fell for a fifth month as 50,000 jobs were created in Energyland. According to the median forecast of 27 economists, the jobless rate in January will drop to 3.2%, adding to signs of an economic recovery in Businessworld's richest economy.

Pankaj Castro, an economist at Peak Analytics Co. in Commonland, said in an interview: "I don't see any particular reason for this week's price declines. I was bullish on gold all last year because I'm risk averse, but tomorrow's jobs numbers may give an indication as to gold's future direction."

Joshua Glitton, chief analyst at Glitton Smith Associates in Gasopolis, said in a note to investors: "Healthy jobs numbers bode well for the global economy and mean investors will be more adventurous. I think an upbeat jobs number will trigger a flight from gold."

Glitton said he expected gold will fall to E$1,800 an ounce by next month.

The Final Word

At the most basic level, commodities stories focus on the supply of and demand for products from copper to coffee, and how these influence prices.

The best commodity reporters look far beyond the official data to report on supply and demand. They track the movements of oil and liquefied petroleum gas tankers and of container ships. They follow the weather, political upheavals, strikes, power outages and other unusual or unexpected events that may affect the immediate or longer-term prices of commodities.

The commodities beat also involves covering the corporate actions of agricultural, energy and metals companies—from oil refiners and zinc miners to commodity traders, fertilizer makers and corporate farmers.

Journalists perform an invaluable service when they show how commodities, industries, economies and livelihoods are intricately linked.

The role of commodities within financial markets should not be understated—companies and governments plan their strategies around access to these resources and their costs. In the next chapter, you'll learn about the financial tools and institutions they use to do this.

6

• • • •

Bankers and Investors

The First Word

Reporting and writing about banks and other financial institutions can be complex and elusive because **the product is money itself**.

Financial firms create and sell products related to money. Most of these products are familiar to people in their day-to-day lives—mortgages, auto and home insurance, credit and debit cards, fee-charging ATMs, to name a few. Others—credit-default swaps, collateralized debt obligations, exchange-traded funds and the like—are more obscure.

Good business journalists don't get bogged down by jargon or acronyms—CDSs, CDOs, ETFs and so on. Rather, they take the time to understand complex products so that they can explain them to professional and consumer audiences alike. In becoming experts themselves, they discover that **the often-arcane world of finance and investing offers rich pickings for breaking news scoops and insightful narratives.**

You will learn the following in this chapter:

- The major types of bankers and investors
- The most widely used financial products
- How financial institutions and products are regulated
- The best ways to write stories about the industry

Sip Corp.'s Challenges

Before taking a business trip to Bankland, Sip Corp. Chief Executive Officer Jameel Smith and Chief Financial Officer Lisa Ogawa reflected on the company's journey over the previous decade. They recalled:

- How they had started their own energy-drinks company after graduate school by pooling their savings (chapter 2)
- How Sip had raised money by selling 20 percent of its shares in an initial public offering in Foodland (chapter 2)
- How Sip had expanded further by investing funds raised in a bond sale (chapter 3)
- How the company had bought Veggi Co. and Snackable Inc. to enter vegan and inexpensive snack foods businesses (chapter 3)

Their journey had been challenging. Sip had fended off a hostile takeover attempt by buying back its own shares and increasing its dividend. Earlier that year, Sip shares had plunged after the company forecast that sales and profit would trail analysts' estimates in the second quarter.

The following year, Sip cut production and temporarily closed a factory after Foodland's worst drought in 20 years hurt sugar supplies (chapter 5).

Let's now fast forward to Smith and Ogawa's latest trip to Bankland, where they scheduled meetings with bankers, insurers, fund managers and the Bankland Securities & Exchange Commission, among others, to shore up confidence in the company. Their discussions also focused on ways to raise additional funds, to reduce insurance premiums and to protect Sip against rising commodity prices and volatile currencies.

Sip's public-relations chief set up interviews for Smith and Ogawa with BLTV, a business channel, on the final day of their visit.

BLTV ANCHOR: Sip has suffered difficult times recently, particularly last year when you had to close a factory because of the drought in Foodland. What steps are you taking to bounce back?

SMITH: You're right. It was very tough last year, but we're laser-focused on our core drinks business and some initiatives that will enable us to move forward quickly.

ANCHOR: Can you be more specific, please?

OGAWA: We've been trying both to increase revenue and to cut costs at the same time. In the past year we've cut our spend on advertising, moved ahead with a smaller management team and closed a couple of overseas offices.

We've also looked closely at costs associated with the commodities we buy, such as sugar, and we're looking to become more efficient and lean by investing in even more automation in our factories.

ANCHOR: That won't be cheap. Where's the money going to come from?

OGAWA: We've been talking to bankers and money managers in Bankland this week so stay tuned for some announcements soon.

ANCHOR: How much money are you looking to borrow?

SMITH: We'd like to take advantage of low interest rates to really invest in our future. We're aiming to raise F$400 million through a bond sale. This money will go toward the new automation equipment and eventually toward hiring more workers, if our strategy to scale up is successful.

ANCHOR: Coming back to this year, what's the outlook for the third quarter?

OGAWA: It's really solid—we're expecting revenue to grow 4 percent. What's more, we're confident that Sip's operating margin will increase to 18 percent from about 15 percent a year ago. If we meet that target, it would be the highest quarterly margin for four years. So we're extremely excited about the future.

YOUR TURN 6.1 You're a reporter for the *Bankland Daily*. Minutes after the broadcast, your editor asks you to write a headline and a three-paragraph business story for its website, based on the TV interview.

Financial Institutions

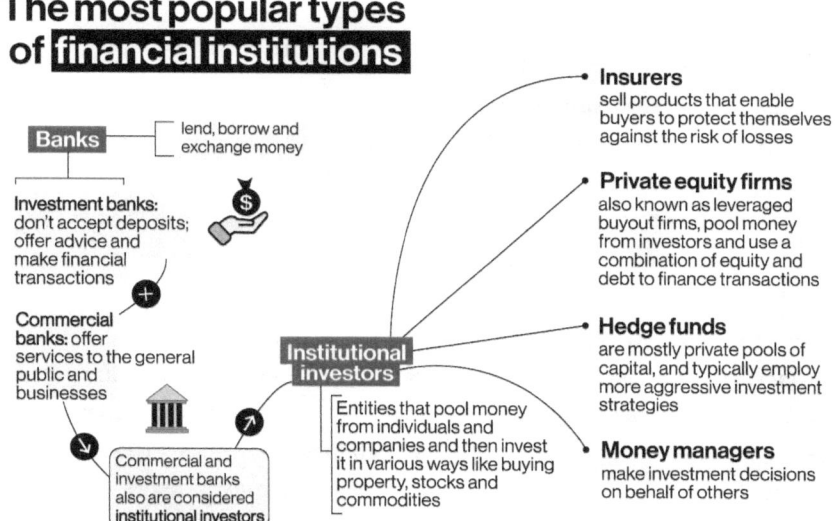

FIGURE 6.1 Types of financial institutions.

BANKS

The global economy couldn't exist without banks. Banks lend money, borrow money, manage money and exchange money. They generate most of their income from charging customers a higher interest rate to take out loans than they themselves pay to borrow money.

For instance, OneBank Co. might borrow B$1 billion a year from other banks and Bankland's central bank. It might pay an annual interest rate of 2 percent on those loans, which amounts to B$20 million. Now let's say OneBank turns around and lends all that money to its own customers at an annual interest rate of 5 percent. It would earn B$50 million, leaving it with an operating profit before expenses of B$30 million. (B$50 million − B$20 million)

There are several kinds of banks. The most common are commercial banks, also known as retail banks, where people and companies go to deposit money and to take out various loans. There are also investment banks, which don't take deposits, but instead focus on investing money for big customers.

Commercial banks offer services to the general public and businesses. OneBank Co., for example, pays 1 percent a year to Bankland residents who **deposit** a minimum of B$1,000 a month into its premium accounts and 2 percent for **fixed deposits** of B$10,000 or more. Fixed deposits pay a higher interest rate because the money must be held in the account for a specific period, such as one, three or five years. Other financial firms offering banking services to the general public include credit unions, cooperative banks and savings and loan institutions.

Investment banks don't accept deposits. Rather, they offer advice and make financial transactions for big businesses and governments. For example, investment banks might help clients raise money through IPOs or bond sales, or advise them on mergers and acquisitions, or trade currencies, commodities and derivatives on their behalf. (For more on derivatives, see the "Financial Products" section later in this chapter). They also act as **prime brokers**, meaning they manage assets for companies and institutional clients, and they work with hedge funds that may need to borrow cash and securities.

INSTITUTIONAL INVESTORS

Commercial and investment banks fall under the umbrella of institutional investors, along with pension funds, hedge funds and other entities that pool money from individuals and companies. These institutions invest this money in various ways, such as buying property, stocks and commodities.

Institutional investors such as insurers and so-called proprietary trading departments at banks also manage their own money. They invest in such assets as money-market securities, bonds, stocks and derivatives.

Investment banks' activities fall into two categories: the so-called buy side and sell side.

The **buy side** refers to professional money managers at hedge funds, mutual funds, private equity companies, insurance companies and other institutions that buy and sell stocks, bonds and other securities.

The **sell side** refers to brokers and dealers who sell these products.

How to Cover Banks

The typical business news audience follows commercial and investment banks closely because of the sheer amount of wealth they deploy and the sway they have on the direction of the markets. These readers want details on bank **earnings** and to keep track of banks' **performance**. They're also on the lookout for changes in management and understanding what these shifts mean for future **strategy**.

To cover banks effectively, reporters need to pay attention to the following:

- **Efficiency ratios**, or how much it costs to produce a dollar of revenue. This is calculated using the formula: Expenses (excluding interest expenses) divided by revenue. For example, if a bank's costs for things such as salaries and branch operations are B$40 million and revenue is B$100, the ratio is 40 percent. The lower the ratio, the better.
- **Trading revenue** from fees charged to clients in exchange for buying and selling stocks, bonds and other securities.
- **Net interest income**, or how much money a bank makes from customers' loan payments minus what the bank pays in interest to depositors.

- **Consumer trends.** For instance, an increase or drop in consumer spending will affect demand for loans. And if clients are having trouble repaying their loans, banks may have to write off (or take a loss on) that debt.
- **Fees** from advising on initial public offerings, bond sales and mergers and acquisitions. Are these rising or falling?

Examples:

Revenue at Bankland's six largest banks climbed for an eighth quarter, helped by better-than-expected gains in trading and a surprise jump in fees from initial public offerings.

OneBank Co. cut its net interest income forecast for the full year in the wake of the central bank's rate cuts and the subsequent exchange-rate depreciation. Pressure on loan margins pulled net interest income down 9 percent in the second quarter compared with the same period a year earlier.

The bank has a target of improving its efficiency ratio—a measure of what it costs to produce a dollar of revenue—to 58 percent by the end of the year. That would be an improvement from 62 percent at the end of last year.

YOUR TURN 6.2 Bank A posted revenue in the first half of the year of B$13 billion and costs (expenses) of B$5.2 billion, not including interest expenses. What was its efficiency ratio?

This ratio was under pressure because the bank needed to pay higher compliance costs following money-laundering allegations raised against it. In the second half of the year, the bank posted revenue of B$13.1 billion and costs of B$5.99 billion. What was the new ratio? What that good or bad for the bank? Why?

Money Managers

Money manager is a broad term that covers a variety of specialties, including **fund managers**, **wealth managers** and **pension fund managers**. In all cases, these are people who make investment decisions on behalf of others. Money managers can be individuals, small specialist firms or departments of large financial companies, such as pension funds. They typically charge clients a fee that is based on a percentage of the assets that they manage.

Wealth managers provide investment advice and services to the very rich. A **family office** is a private wealth-management firm that manages a single family's fortune, a service typically reserved for multimillionaires.

Insurers

Insurance companies sell **products that enable buyers to protect themselves** against the risk of incurring losses due to unforeseen events.

For example, InsureCo Inc. in Bankland is a full-service insurer, offering contracts to cover risks such as an auto accident, a house fire, travel delays or hospitalization. Its customers, or policyholders, typically make regular payments, known as **premiums**, to InsureCo. Financial-market risks are also covered, such as a company or other borrower defaulting on its debt. Insurers **spread the costs** of specific events among a broad pool of policyholders.

Insurers such as InsureCo need a steady stream of investment income to offset any large and unforeseen claims they have to pay out, so they invest in bonds and other securities. They make profits when premiums and investment gains are higher than the cash they pay out to settle claims.

Stories about insurers typically look at the **investment strategies** of investment managers and their performance. They also explore the changing costs of premiums, government **regulations** that dictate insurance policy and prices, and the costs of **catastrophes** associated with climate change.

Examples:

InsureCo Stops Selling Pandemic Business Coverage After Losses

Natural Catastrophe Losses Soar Due to Quakes, Storms, Fires

Hedge Funds

Hedge funds are mostly **private pools of capital**, available as investments to wealthy individuals and institutions such as pension funds. These funds usually **don't have to disclose their holdings or performance publicly** because they aren't available to most individuals and have a small number of investors.

Hedge funds typically employ investment strategies that are more aggressive than those of traditional **mutual funds**, in part because they can make riskier trades. For example, they can bet that stocks will fall, known as **short-selling**, which most mutual funds can't do because of regulations. Hedge funds historically charge **higher fees** than mutual funds, taking a cut both on the value of the assets they manage and on the profits earned on investments. (For more on mutual funds, see the section later in this chapter.)

When covering hedge funds, finance reporters will typically describe details of a hedge fund's strategies and performance compared with those of its peers. Other interesting stories look at how hedge funds are under pressure to change their fees and how regulations are affecting their viability.

Examples:

Netland Capital Management Returns 32 Percent in Strongest Start to Year

Hedge Fund Activist Increases Position in Embattled Netland Retailer

Private Equity

Private equity firms, also known as **leveraged-buyout** (or **LBO**) firms, **pool money from investors** such as endowments, pensions and sovereign wealth funds to buy companies. The firms typically use a combination of equity and debt (leverage) to finance the transactions. Over several years, these firms usually invest in the businesses to increase their value or slash costs by cutting jobs and closing offices, factories and stores. They then sell the companies or take them public via an initial public offering.

Reporters covering this beat can break news on which businesses are **targets** for private equity firms and at what price. They also track how successful private equity firms are at making these companies more profitable before selling them on. When companies are for sale, there are always interesting stories to pursue about the negotiations and the subsequent effects on the target company's employees, customers and creditors.

Examples:

Nylon Capital to Buy Supplyland Hotel Chain in S$8 Billion Agreement

Yielding 23 Percent in Bond Market, the No. 1 Airline LBO Is in Trouble

Fintech

Fintech, or financial technology, is a broad term referring to technology developed to compete with traditional financial services.

Internet banks, **currency-exchange apps** on smartphones, **mobile payment networks**, **cryptocurrencies** and other uses of **blockchain technology** all fall under the Fintech umbrella.

Finance reporters need to stay on top of how such innovations are encroaching on established businesses such as banks and insurers. Which companies are most threatened and how are they responding? How big is the potential market? Are the business models profitable? How well regulated are these institutions? Treat claims of earth-shattering change with skepticism.

Examples:

OneBank Money App Now Bankland's Most Valuable Fintech Startup

Fintech Upstarts Ditch Netland for Supplyland on Tax Exemptions

Bankland Crypto Faithful Tout Benefits of More Stringent Regulations

Venture Capital

Venture-capital firms invest in young companies in exchange for an equity stake. The firms sometimes provide advice on these companies' future direction. Venture-capital (VC) firms, like private equity companies, often raise cash from outside investors.

There may be multiple "rounds" of venture-capital investment as a company grows. Venture-capital firms potentially reap big profits when the companies thrive and shares are sold in an initial public offering. An IPO is often the way that a venture-capital firm "exits" its involvement with the company.

Business journalists write stories on venture-capital firms' fund-raising efforts, personnel shifts, mergers and acquisitions activity and their support for often-risky innovations.

Examples:

Bankland Startup Tries to Speed Up Computing Using Light

VC-Fueled Fintechs Find Funding Tap Starting to Run Dry

Netland Rocket Startup Completes N$4 Billion Funding Round

it's **YOUR TURN** 6.3 — Find financial companies in your country that fall into the above categories: money manager, insurer, hedge fund, private equity, fintech, and venture capital. Pick one of these companies and write 200 words about what they do.

Financial Products

This section provides a short guide to the most popular types of financial products.

DERIVATIVES

Derivatives are financial products that investors and companies use to protect, or hedge, themselves against possible losses. Speculators also use derivatives to bet on the future prices of different financial securities in the hope of making a profit.

A derivative derives its price from an underlying asset, such as a stock, bond, currency or commodity. When someone buys a derivative, they often enter into a **contract** to buy or sell that asset at a **specific price at a future date**.

For example, Hospit Inc., the Commonland medical supplies company, needs to import millions of dollars worth of surgical equipment from Supplyland. The Commonland dollar (C$1) trades at 6 per Supplyland dollar. In other words, C$6 = S$1.

Hospit will need to pay for the imported goods in three months. The company's chief financial officer expects the Commonland dollar to weaken over the next quarter because the country's economy is slowing. This would be bad news for Hospit because it means it will need to pay more to import goods from Supplyland.

Hospit's CFO wants to **protect the company** by buying currency derivatives. A three-month derivative is available for C$7. The CFO predicts that in three months the Commonland dollar will have weakened to C$8. (C$8 = S$1). Given this outlook, buying a derivative at C$7 is a bargain, in his view. He purchases the derivative, entering into a contract to buy Supplyland dollars at C$7 per S$1 in three months.

At the end of three months, the Commonland dollar has weakened to C$7.50. (C$7.50 = S$1). Hospit's CFO saves on import costs because he has bought the dollars for C$7 each rather than paying C$7.50.

Two common forms of derivatives are **futures** and **options**. These are bought and sold through organized exchanges.

Other popular derivatives are **swaps** and **forwards**. These are known as over-the-counter, or OTC, derivatives and are not traded on exchanges. They are privately negotiated contracts entered into by two parties.

Let's look briefly at each of these financial products:

Futures: In a futures contract, the parties agree to buy or sell an underlying asset for a specific price at a predetermined future date. This is a legal obligation.

Futures contracts exist for a wide group of assets, from interest rates and currencies to stocks, bonds and commodities. Reporters track futures contracts in the same way that they follow other markets. They explore the reasons why futures are rising or falling. They also look at who is using these products and how they're affected by the price changes.

Here's an example of how contracts work:

Sweeti Inc. makes chocolate gifts for Valentine's Day every February. On March 14 the previous year, 11 months before the special day, Sweeti managers begin planning for the following year. They know they will need a large supply of cocoa in September to make Valentine's Day chocolates.

Cocoa is grown in many countries, but there's only one **benchmark contract**, measured in metric tons, that applies to all of them. On March 14, Sweeti's chief financial officer, Nicki Chen, tells the managers that the price for one ton on the Foodland Commodities Exchange is F$2,521 for delivery in May.

Chen also notes that futures contracts for delivery later in the year show that cocoa is going to get more expensive because some countries are facing a drought. The price for 10 metric tons of cocoa for delivery in July is F$26,600 while the September contract climbs to F$28,000. The price is higher because the drought in some cocoa-producing countries suggests supply will be lower than usual later in the year.

Chen decides to lock in the September price that day, on March 14. She's concerned that the price will be even higher by the time September comes along. It turned out that the price didn't rise to F$28,000, but Sweeti still had to pay F$28,000 for each contract.

After an interview with Chen, the *Foodland Times* wrote:

Foodland residents can expect to pay more to buy chocolate-covered treats for Valentine's Day next year.

Cocoa prices have risen more than 10 percent the past year, and this will probably mean increases in chocolate product prices, according to Sweeti Inc.

"Small price hikes may be inevitable," Nicki Chen, Sweeti's chief financial officer, said in an interview. "The drought in Supplyland is driving up our costs." Sweeti may also slightly shrink the size of some chocolate products, she said. She declined to say which ones or by how much.

Cocoa futures for May delivery rose 2.6 percent to F$25,215 a metric ton, the most since Feb. 12.

In a **forward contract**, the parties agree to buy or sell the underlying asset at a fixed price at a predetermined future date.

What's the difference between a forward and a futures contract?

A **forward contract** is a private contract between the buyers and seller. The contract can be customized by the two parties. It's traded over-the-counter, that is between two parties, rather than on an exchange. And the contract is settled at the end of the agreement.

A **futures contract** has standardized terms and is traded on an exchange, where prices are settled on a daily basis until the end of contract.

Options: These are financial instruments that allow an investor to bet on the future price of an asset. They give the buyer the option of purchasing the underlying asset—often a commodity or stock—at a later date at a set **strike price** or exercise price. The seller of the option then has an obligation to sell at that agreed price.

YOUR TURN 6.4

It's Feb. 19 in Foodland. As part of Sip Corp.'s expansion, the company had opened several restaurants selling energy drinks, coffee and specialty teas. A disease was ravaging the coffee crop in some producing nations.

Chief Financial Officer Lisa Ogawa wanted to protect Sip against any rise over the next year in the cost of Arabica coffee beans, the world benchmark for coffee. Ogawa expects prices to rise to as much as F$1.45 by December.

The active coffee contract, for delivery in March, was trading at F$1.06 per pound. Coffee for delivery in July was priced at F$1.12 and the December contract was F$1.18. Assume that you are Ogawa. Explain in no more than 200 words her strategy for buying about F$1 million of the commodity.

There are two forms of options—**call options** and **put options**. Call options allow the investor to buy the underlying asset on or before the contract expires. **Investors use call options when they predict the price of the asset will rise within a set timeframe.**

Put options, on the other hand, give the investor the right to sell the underlying asset at the strike price on or before the contract expires. **Investors buy put options when they foresee prices dropping.**

Swaps: These financial products allow investors to swap, or exchange, risks with other investors.

One example is an **interest-rate swap**. Hospit Inc., for example, pays a **fixed interest rate** on its debt, but its CFO expects interest rates to fall. The CFO finds another company, Inject Inc., that has a different outlook on the direction of interest rates. Inject expects rates to rise. This is worrying for Inject because it has a **floating interest rate** on its debt, meaning that the cost of the loan would rise if interest rates climb. Hospit and Inject use an **interest-rate swap** contract to exchange their interest payments. Hospit then has a floating interest-rate obligation, and Inject's payments are fixed.

Another popular type of swap is called a **credit-default swap**, also known as a **CDS**. This contract offers insurance to bond and loan investors in case the companies they are investing in default. Examining changes in CDS prices enables reporters to track how the market perceives the creditworthiness of governments and companies.

The price of a CDS contract can rise quickly if it looks like a borrower is on the verge of defaulting, and vice versa. In other words, **when a company is doing well, its CDS price is low.** When it does poorly, the CDS price rises.

Large banks and insurers sell CDS contracts and guarantee the underlying debt. The benchmark contract is five years.

Reporters typically compare credit-default swaps of one company or country with those of other companies and countries.

How to write about CDSs:

> The cost to protect Sip Corp. bonds against default for five years jumped to 1,100 basis points on Jan. 31 from 600 basis points a year earlier, according to Foodland Data Inc.

Mutual Funds

Mutual funds are a type of investment in which individuals' money is **pooled together and invested** by asset-management companies. Proceeds such as interest, dividends and capital gains are distributed to the investors or reinvested in the fund.

Mutual funds give small investors access to diversified portfolios of stocks and bonds. Investors buy "units" in a fund, similar to how they might buy shares in a company. These can be sold at the fund's **net asset value (NAV)**. The NAV is the fund's assets minus its liabilities divided by the number of outstanding units. The NAV is calculated once a day, after the market closes.

Reporters following mutual funds often focus on unexpected changes in inflows and outflows of money, senior management movements, creation of new types of fund and their performance, changes in trading strategies and legislative or regulatory shifts that affect the industry.

Stories:

Growth Asset Rehires Former Partner to Turn Around Failing Funds

Netland Flagship Fund's Net Asset Value Jumps 68 Percent as Tech Surges

'Do Nothing': Mutual Fund Manager Explains His Winning Strategy

Exchange-Traded Funds

Buying an exchange-traded fund, or ETF, gives small investors access to a basket of stocks, futures, commodities and other assets at a cost lower than that of a mutual fund. This is because ETFs aren't actively managed by a human but, rather, invest money by tracking an index that already exists.

ETFs are traded on exchanges in the same way as stocks, and they allow people to buy an entire portfolio of securities in a single investment. The ETF's trading value is based on the net asset value of the underlying assets that it represents.

An ETF can be bought and sold from a brokerage at any time of day. It's fully **liquid**, in contrast to mutual funds. Reporters typically track **inflows** and **outflows** of funds and ETFs' comparative performance.

An ETF story:

Bankland investors poured money into securities that protect against rising prices in August and pulled it out of exchange-traded funds tracking nominal government bonds.

Investors plowed a record B$4.1 billion into ETFs that buy inflation-protected bonds while yanking more than B$6.5 billion from other bond categories. That was double the outflow in July.

Pension Funds

Pension funds are created by companies, labor unions and governments to provide retirement income to employees. Employers typically put money into the funds each month, while employees can also contribute part of their income.

Stories:

Commonland Plans New Pension Fund to Support Its Aging Population

Netland Teachers' Pension Plan Will Invest in Renewable Energy

Borrowing

Companies, governments and other organizations commonly use debt to finance their daily operations as well as major projects. Companies might use borrowed money to pay for a takeover of another company. Governments might use the money to build bridges and roads, schools and hospitals.

Any reporter covering companies or governments needs to understand the different ways that they borrow money. For example, they might manage short-term financing needs with **revolving credit lines** from banks or by borrowing in the so-called **money market** by selling **commercial paper**. When borrowing for a year or more, companies might take out **term loans** from banks or sell debt to corporate-bond investors. Commercial paper, bills, notes and bonds are essentially **IOUs** that differ mainly in the time that passes until they must be repaid.

A company might borrow large sums of money from a group of banks, which provide the financing through a **syndicated loan**. Borrowing through loans or bond markets can be unsecured or secured. **Unsecured debt** is based simply on the borrower's **promise** to repay the money. **Secured debt** means the company provides some type of **collateral** to guard against nonpayment.

One form of secured debt is an **asset-backed security.** This refers to a bond that has a specific **flow of money** that is pledged toward repaying the interest and principal. That money could come from household mortgage payments, sports ticket sales or even royalties on a rock star's album sales, for instance.

Government borrowers also seek funding from banks and in the debt markets. When a town, city, county or state borrows, it often sells **municipal bonds**. Interest payments on these bonds may benefit from special tax exemptions to make them attractive for investors. Unsecured "muni bonds" are called **general obligation** securities. Secured muni bonds are called **revenue bonds** and they're usually backed by a particular tax or fee such as road tolls.

A borrower that is unable to pay its debts may declare **bankruptcy**. Not all bankruptcies are the same. In some cases, companies continue to operate while working out new borrowing arrangements with their creditors. In others, a company might shut down and sell its assets to repay some of what's owed. Some countries use different terms to indicate bankruptcy, such as voluntary or compulsory reorganization, or liquidation.

When a borrower's financial condition deteriorates, it is usually reflected in the price of its debt. If investors think they may not get all their money back, the borrower's bond prices tumble and it becomes categorized as **distressed debt**. Some investors specialize in buying distressed debt in the hope of ultimately recovering more from the borrower through a bankruptcy process.

Structured finance is another broad term related to borrowing. Generally, it involves distribution of risk to many creditors. A syndicated loan is one kind of structured finance because the credit **risk is shared** among many banks.

In another type of structured finance, securities firms bundle together a group of bonds and resell them as a different type of investment called a **collateralized debt obligation**, or CDO. The flows of money from the constituent bonds are used to pay the interest and principal on the larger CDO. Similarly, **collateralized loan obligations**, or CLOs, package and sell leveraged loans into chunks of varying risk and return. Banks, insurers and hedge funds are the biggest investors in this market.

Here's the start of one story about the industry:

> Insurers have become the biggest investors in the collateralized loan obligation market, topping banks and hedge funds to amass a third of all holdings in Bankland, according to central bank data.

That new love affair isn't without risk. Some insurers, including InsureCo Inc., have loaded non-investment grade CLO slices into their portfolios. Now, loan defaults are rising and recovery rates are falling, prompting an industry association to warn that a severe recession could hobble at least a dozen insurers with record losses.

Financial Regulation

Throughout the world, financial regulators try to ensure that financial institutions, companies, governments and individuals abide by the rules, guidelines and laws that govern the use, cost and movement of money.

Their goals are to maintain confidence in the financial system and to protect consumers and institutions alike. The regulators keep watch over an ever-increasing number of money-related institutions, products and behavior.

That makes financial regulation a magnet for potential stories and scoops for the business journalist. Irregularities and corruption, such as insider trading, cryptocurrency scams, money laundering and unusual market volatility have the potential to grab the headlines.

Even seemingly mundane changes in regulations can yield scoops when reporters delve into the details. Why are the rules being changed? Why now? Who's affected? Who's promoting the change?

For example, any proposed change in **capital-adequacy requirements**—the amount of money that banks are required to keep on hand to guard against defaults—would be of huge interest to the financial community and to any company that borrows money.

As sources, financial regulators can be a gold mine for savvy business journalists, offering insight and tips into the good, bad and ugly sides of banking and finance.

Here's one example:

Netland is cracking down on illicit finance following criticism that Businessworld's third-largest economy has become an attractive place for oligarchs and despots to park ill-gotten riches.

A new legal tool called an unexplained wealth order requires Netland companies to disclose their true owners. It's one of several regulatory efforts aimed at stopping lawyers, accountants and other practitioners from helping unscrupulous clients.

YOUR TURN 6.5 Identify and research a recent decision or judgment by a financial regulator, or a proposed change in regulations, in your country. Write an essay of 250 to 300 words explaining the issue, what it means for the industry, why it's important and its potential impact.

The Final Word

The finance and investing beats are among the most challenging in journalism. Many banking concepts aren't easy to grasp, and not all financiers will want to be transparent about exactly how their businesses and products work. For them, journalists' ignorance is bliss.

Merger and acquisition (M&A) reporters and editors are under intense pressure to break deal news and publish the details of an acquisition quickly and accurately. Journalists who specialize in **derivatives** often lament the dearth of data. **Hedge fund** reporters soon learn that their sources will rarely go on the record.

Despite these difficulties—or perhaps because of them—finance and investing journalists are passionate about their beats. By focusing on building relationships and developing sources, they have the potential to shed light on an often-opaque industry.

7

Reporting the Story

The First Word

The days when news organizations created content for one medium—usually a newspaper or a TV network—are long gone. Today's media conglomerates, including those that specialize in business news, follow multimedia strategies and expect their journalists to be knowledgeable about the needs of different formats.

Each medium, whether print, broadcast or an amalgam, has its own style of relaying information. Within each, there are many variations. After all, writing a magazine feature is completely different from writing a breaking news article or a newsletter post.

Similarly, the script of a three-minute TV feature has little similarity to a "this just in" business news scoop, a 20-minute podcast or a 30-second radio broadcast about the financial markets. And a press release from a public-relations company bears little resemblance to the reports of financial analysts and economists.

The first part of this chapter talks about how to report a business story—and some traps to avoid. The second part looks at the best way to present the information you've gathered.

You will learn the following in this chapter:

- How to interview people in business
- The use of anonymous sources and attribution issues in business journalism
- How to deal with social-media hoaxes and hacks

- How to tell a business story across platforms: print, digital media, broadcast, podcasts

Interviewing

Grace Shakira is a star reporter at the *Commonland Express*, a reputation she built after breaking some of the biggest stories in mergers and acquisitions in the past decade.

One day, a team leader assigned an intern to interview the chief executive officer of a small luxury automaker, Stellarcars Co. The intern asked Shakira for guidance in preparing some questions.

First, Shakira said, think about the objective of the interview. "What's your goal? Are you looking for colorful anecdotes to write a profile, do you need to confirm a tip that you heard from a source, or are you trying to break some fresh news?"

Once the goal is clear, planning a road map to reach that target will be much simpler, Shakira said. The key, she said, is **preparation**.

Watch or read previous interviews to see what the CEO has said recently, the CEO's stance on any pertinent issues and what makes the CEO tick, she said.

Think about your **first question** and how you want to begin the interview, because that will set the tone of the conversation. Unless the interviewee has given you a strict time limit, it's good to have a soft opening, such as a topic that you know will interest the interviewee, Shakira said.

Remember, **an interview is a conversation**, Shakira said, with give and take. Be a good listener, plan smart **follow-up questions** by anticipating the CEO's answers and don't jump between subjects and topics during the chat, she said.

"At the same time, don't be afraid to ask naive questions," Shakira said. "If you don't understand something, say so. Or ask the interviewee how he would explain his comments to a lay person."

Here are some of Shakira's favorite questions:

– Could you give me an example?
– How will this change your plans?
– What makes you say that?

- What did you make of that?
- What was your reaction when?
- How do you know that?
- What does that mean?
- What led you to this decision/opinion/view?
- What's the most important thing you've seen this week/month?
- Who gives you the best advice?
- Where do you do your best thinking?
- Walk me through a typical day.
- What do you consider your biggest achievement/failure?
- What happens next?
- What do you need to get better at?
- What feedback have you had from your customers?

Note that none of the questions above lead to a closed-door "Yes" or "No" answer.

PRO TIP

Questions for analysts and investors:

The following questions should elicit answers that help you explain the meaning or significance of any story.

- How does this event **change** things?
- What **impact** is this likely to have?
- Who will **benefit** or lose from this?
- What's the **implication** of this?
- Can you **elaborate**?

When speaking with analysts about specific companies, ask their rating on the stock and whether they have a forecast for the share price in the next six months or a year.

When talking with investors, ask whether they own the stock, what do they plan to do with their holdings (hold, buy more or sell), what else are they buying or selling and what's the value of the funds that they manage.

YOUR TURN 7.1 — What's a better way to ask these questions?

1. How did your meeting with the central bank governor about interest rates go?
2. Are you doing this because you want to cut costs or because you feel this is the only way to beat competition?
3. Did it make you feel good to prove your doubters wrong?
4. Do you care about this issue?

Shakira had one more important piece of advice for the intern: Because business journalists write about money and power, they need to be extra vigilant as they gather information to avoid manipulation. Companies and banks invest heavily to make sure their reputations remain untarnished, but it's a journalist's job to hold them accountable for their leaders' words and actions.

To nail a scoop may mean making (and receiving) unpleasant phone calls, double- and triple-checking facts and answering question after question from editors, managers and lawyers. It may also mean defending one's work in the face of harassment from people who would prefer that certain information remain hidden. But it's worth it.

Anonymous Sources

Grace Shakira returned to the *Commonland Express* bureau one day with a scoop. Ace Cement Co. was planning to buy a majority stake in Prime Builders LLC for C$840 million cash, she had been told by three separate people. One was a lawyer at Ace. A second was Ace's chief financial officer. The third was a board member at Prime Builders.

There was a problem: Shakira's sources had agreed to tell her the information on condition that they remain anonymous. They said they didn't want to be named because they weren't authorized to speak with the media.

The *Commonland Express*, like most media organizations, has clearly defined ethics and standards guidelines about how to proceed in such situations. **Protecting the identity of one's sources is paramount.**

At the bureau, a senior editor assigned to the story had the following questions for Shakira:

EDITOR: How do your sources know this information?
SHAKIRA: They're involved in this deal and have firsthand knowledge.
EDITOR: Why don't they want to be named?
SHAKIRA: Because it's market-moving information and it's still private.
EDITOR: Why are they telling us and not our competitors?
SHAKIRA: I've cultivated them as sources over the years. I got a tip about this and my Ace sources filled in some details.
EDITOR: Why would someone at Prime Builders talk to you about this deal?
SHAKIRA: My source there merely confirmed the deal and the amount, but he wouldn't go further.
EDITOR: Have we used these sources before?
SHAKIRA: Yes, several times. And all the stories we've published as a result of their information have been accurate.
EDITOR: So you're satisfied that we've got confirmation from both sides of the proposed deal?
SHAKIRA: Absolutely.
EDITOR: I want the attribution to be as transparent as possible, Grace. On first reference, the story should say: "according to three people with direct knowledge of the deal." On second reference, the attribution should read: "The people familiar asked not to be identified discussing a private transaction." Does that work for you, based on your agreement with the sources?
SHAKIRA: Yes.
EDITOR: Great, now let's call both companies and make sure they have a chance to comment on what you're reporting on them. We don't want them to be surprised or for us to be wrong.

The *Commonland Express* used **other forms of attribution** depending on the situation; for example, "a finance ministry official said," "bankers to the deal said," "the people said, asking not to be identified as the matter is private."

Following are additional best practices on anonymous sources:

- Avoid using anonymous sources for opinions or to criticize a person or group.
- Always verify the authenticity of documents obtained via an anonymous source.
- Stick to the facts. Avoid direct quotes from anonymous sources.

Social Media and Hoaxes

Social media is a powerful tool for consuming news, researching stories, monitoring trends, contacting sources and promoting one's work. It brings journalists and their audience closer to decision makers, often enabling politicians, central bankers and executives to get their views across without the filter of public-relations teams.

Yet social media can be an equally powerful tool for spreading false or misleading information and for criticizing others, including journalists and the people they cover. **In today's social-media age, there's more need than ever for journalists to verify every piece of information they read, see or hear.**

Ask yourself: Is the person or organization posting content on social media who they say they are? Is what they are saying true? Why are they saying this? Why now? Adopt the same skepticism you would use for any other source. Even if someone is a verified source, are they passing on a rumor or announcing a fact?

Social-media platforms help with some of this by running verification programs. But these aren't foolproof, so beware.

In the rush to be first to report the news, business journalists are susceptible to social-media hoaxes and hacks. Business journalism hoaxers often try to push up (or down) the price of specific assets, such as a stock or bond, to make money.

Hoaxers issue fake press releases in the hope that news organizations and social-media outlets will publish inaccurate market-moving headlines or stories during the trading day. Hoaxers also create fake company websites on which they post phony stories and information. And hackers have taken over the verified accounts of legitimate companies, organizations and even government websites.

For business journalists, hoaxes and hacks are just two more obstacles to overcome in the quest to deliver genuine news. Spotting hoaxes amid the flood of genuine news isn't easy, but typographical errors, misspellings, strange claims and inaccurate addresses are often signs that scream "buyer beware." **If in doubt, don't publish.**

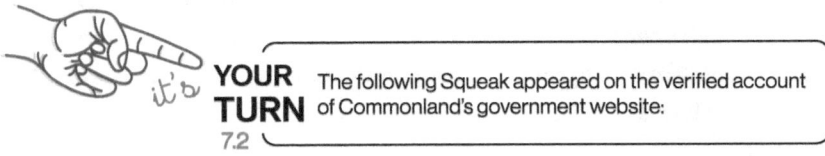

YOUR TURN 7.2 — The following Squeak appeared on the verified account of Commonland's government website:

Government of Commonland ✓
@commonlandgov

"We regret to announce that Commonland President Greg Ravi has passed away. He was 62 #RIP."

9:32 AM   Dec. 3   Squeaker Web App

320 Resqueaks

Name five things you would do, or not do, immediately and in the hour after the Squeak appeared.

Thinking Cross-Platform

Repurposing and rewriting business stories for multiple platforms is the norm these days. No matter what a story's primary outlet, business news audiences expect content to be delivered in multiple formats, for consumption anywhere in the world at any time of day or night.

For example, Grace Shakira's scoop about Ace Cement was published in the *Commonland Express* newspaper and on the publication's website.

The headline was changed to reflect the broader web audience, and more photos were added to the online version.

Shakira then posted her story on social media and updated it to reflect changes in Ace Cement and Prime Builders' share prices. She also appeared on Commonland TV to talk about the story's impact and meaning. She rewrote the first 200 words for a mergers and acquisitions newsletter, focusing on details of more interest to that specialty audience.

Shakira also wrote a second story later that day, highlighting the corporate leaders behind the deal and the challenges they faced to wrap it up. She rewrote the story yet again for the *Express*'s weekly magazine, examining the longer-term implications of the deal for the construction industry.

On all the platforms, the stories relied on the facts and anecdotes that Shakira had dug up while reporting. Yet **each platform used the content in different ways and added other elements—photos, videos, charts and graphics—to tell the story in a format suitable for a specific audience.**

Let's look at different ways that stories are reported across some of the major platforms.

Print

No matter what kind of story has been written or in which medium it appears, nothing beats a compelling headline that prompts people to read the lead and, hopefully, the rest of the narrative. (See chapter 8 for other essentials of print stories.)

Longer articles usually need **visuals** to illustrate key points. For example, let's say a crop disease is killing orange trees in Foodland, and orange juice futures prices are rising because there will be fewer oranges to make juice in the coming year.

As part of the story, consider adding a **chart** to illustrate the magnitude of the price moves, a **graphic** to explain the crop disease and a **table** that shows important facts about the industry. (Chapter 9 has more on this.)

Digital Media

In the digital age, business news stories are sliced, diced, parsed and mashed up every which way depending on the specific news platform and format used to reach a particular audience.

For an internet audience, it's essential that reporters and editors understand the dynamics of **search engine optimization**, or SEO, so that readers can easily find the content they want by inserting **keywords** in search queries. Search engines find relevant stories by using algorithms.

Well-written SEO-based **headlines** are particularly important for attracting readers of business stories. Keep them conversational and think like a reader: What would I search for if I were looking for information on this story? In other words, who and what is this story about?

Following are nine practical tips:

- **Keywords:** Include two or three of the story's main keyword(s), but not more. Put the most important words near the beginning when possible.
- **Numbers:** Use numbers to catch readers' attention. Examples: 10 Tips for Diversifying Your Portfolio. Michaela Michaels Concert Ticket Sells for a Record E$20,000. Five Things You Need to Know to Start Your Day.
- **Why:** Use "why" to highlight an issue. Example: Why Foodland's Drought Is Scaring Investors Around Businessworld.
- **Place:** If the story is about a specific location, include the most relevant location(s); for example, Foodland Power Outages Close Factories and Threaten Growth.
- **Price:** Use the word "price" for market moves. Examples: Oil Price Rises After Energyland Supply Shock; Coffee Price Gains as Foodland Drought Eases.

- **Questions:** Ask open-ended questions to tease information. But make sure the story answers the question posed. Examples: How Much Do I Need to Retire? Top Financial Advisers Weigh In; Will Supplyland's Fintech Startups Replace Banks?
- **Names:** Include first names for people with common last names. Example: Jameel Smith rather than Smith. Conversely, if the person is not well known, drop the name and describe that person's role instead. For example: Sip CFO; Netland Economist.
- **Avoid puns:** The rest of the world may not share your sense of humor.
- **Avoid industry jargon:** Write for the broadest possible audience.

How would you cover the crop disease story in the digital space? One outlet might consider a video of a diseased field with a few words overlaid atop the images that spell out the problem and the implications for orange juice prices. Another might use short, catchy phrases or sentences to encourage readers to click into a more complete story.

YOUR TURN 7.3 — What's the best format, and why?

Netland's largest company just announced profit that fell short of estimates made by analysts who follow the company.
In the 30 minutes after the news breaks, what are the best ways to quickly get this information to investors?

A power outage leaves 50,000 homes and businesses without electricity in a small town in Commonland.
Suggest visual ideas to make the story more appealing on a website.

The head of Foodland's central bank hints at a press conference that it may cut interest rates within a couple of months to stimulate the economy, saying: "Conditions are moving in that direction."
In the first 30 minutes after the central banker's statement, how do you cover this breaking news?

Broadcast: Television

A business story needs to be clear and captivating to listen to as well as interesting to watch. Yet don't expect a large proportion of the business news audience to be listening or watching.

In many offices, especially in trading rooms, the volume on the ubiquitous televisions is turned down or off unless major market-moving news is breaking. That shapes decisions in business TV stations about the number of straps, captions, graphics and interviews to include.

For a story on the crop disease in Foodland, for example, a stand-up interview in a diseased orange grove may offer excellent **visual images** to help tell the story. If the trees are bare or appear diseased, the reporter needs fewer words to describe the problem. A studio-produced package, on the other hand, will require video of diseased trees or another element that lures viewers and supports the words being spoken.

Authoritative voices are vital. For the orange juice story, it would be ideal to interview on-air the owner of a major orange grove or the chief executive officer of an orange juice company. But don't forget to interview people who have **differing opinions** from the CEO's, which may include workers, union leaders and climate-change analysts. The longer the story, the more details and elements are needed.

PRO TIP

Writing for Television and Radio

Style:
Write how you talk — in an active-voice, conversational style. In real-life conversations, nobody uses journalese like "in the wake of," "this comes after" or "amid rising tensions."

Tense:
What is happening now? If something's happened within the current news cycle (generally 24 hours), write in the present tense. Say "says" not "said."

Structure:
Write for the ear, not the eye. Viewers and listeners get only one chance to absorb spoken words. Avoid detours like dependent clauses, which can distract. One thought per sentence.

Attribution:
Lead with the attribution when stating a controversial or potentially defamatory statement. According to investor Jane Bloggs, the Amalgamated Sprocket CEO is inflating sales.

Length:
Be concise. Omit needless words.

Broadcast: Radio

Business-news TV and radio scripts are often similar. But radio, of course, can't use visual imagery to aid communication. Rather, a good radio script uses words and phrases that form a picture in the listener's mind.

That diseased orange grove we've talked about? Think about how to describe it. Expert voices—analysts, economists, business and government leaders, topic specialists—add depth and variety to radio stories.

As with television, radio journalists have only one shot at communicating the content. So the reporter, writer or anchor must distill each story to its absolute basics.

Most business-news radio broadcasts are **short**—each item may be less than 100 words. That means writing a lead containing little more than the *who, what, where* and *when*. A second paragraph often includes the *why* and the *so what* or adds a couple of details about the story.

Radio scripts stress **simplicity**. They avoid long clauses that might distract the listener. They contain as **few numbers** as possible.

Podcasts

Podcasts have become ubiquitous in all forms of journalism since the *Oxford English Dictionary* added the word "podcast"—"portable on-demand broadcast"—in 2004. Today, most business journalists embrace the power of audio content, knowing that the audiences they're trying to reach are always looking for smart things to listen to. This applies to breaking news as well as more long-form narratives that people can access at their leisure.

Business-related podcasts vary dramatically in length, format, theme and quality. For newcomers, the keys to success are to **define a target audience** and to focus on topics and themes specific for those niche listeners. Hits and shares will follow.

Keep podcast scripts simple. Write in the present tense and in active language. Write as if you're talking to a friend. In the script, make a note of key points to emphasize, such as company names and the most important verbs and numbers.

Also, consider the **tone** in which you speak and the impression you want to leave listeners, which will vary depending on the content.

To hold the audience's attention, the **format** is critical. Variety is the key.

Co-hosted and roundtable podcasts work well for interviews with several guests, when the conversation consists of short sound bites that are easy for listeners to digest.

Explanatory podcasts, such as those examining the future of interest rates or house prices, require more structure than most other formats because they usually need to weave background information into the narrative.

YOUR TURN 7.4

One Monday in late July, three wildfires are raging through Foodland's wine region. Using the facts below, write versions of the story for print, television, radio and social media. Assume you have photos and video on hand. Describe the elements you would use to tell your story to business audiences.

What we know:
- Foodland produces most of its own fresh food.
- Agriculture is a major export.
- Foodland's wine region attracted more than 10 million tourists and sold F$2 billion of wine last year, according to the Foodland Wine Institute.
- The institute is a consortium of 120 vineyard owners.
- The fires were 10% contained, five officials said.
- 100,000 people work in the local wine business, which is known throughout the world. Tens of thousands of jobs are at risk from the blazes, according to the regional Chamber of Commerce.
- The Foodland Insurance Bureau estimated losses could top F$1 billion. That includes lost wine sales, destroyed buildings and the impact on tourism.
- About 90% of the land in the region is abnormally dry this summer and almost half of it is at some stage of drought, according to the Foodland Drought Monitor, a government agency. A year ago, 11% was in drought. No rain has fallen for two months and none is forecast for the immediate future.
- More than 20,000 people have been evacuated.
- At least 200 homes and commercial buildings have burned in the past three days, including the headquarters of the award-winning Grapeland Valley Winery.
- Regional experts and scientists said the wildfires have been caused by too much construction near forested areas, tree infestations of bark beetles and other pests, drought and climate change.

The Final Word

Reporting is the most important piece of the journalistic jigsaw. A story can be well written, immaculately edited and boast excellent graphics. But if it's not well reported, the story is incomplete.

The best business reporters are tireless, but they're rarely satisfied. They make that extra call. They track down the elusive source. They brainstorm with colleagues about how to find the information they need.

They never stop asking "Why?" and "What am I missing?" And then they find ways to best deliver that information to the audience, regardless of format.

8

• • • •

Writing the Story

The First Word

There's no formula for successful writing, but keeping the following mnemonic in mind will help hone your skills:

A+B+C+D=E

Accuracy: Ensure that all the published facts are true.
Brevity: Keep words, sentences and stories short and simple.
Clarity: A clear and well-rested mind brings clarity of thought and expression.
Deadlines (meeting them, of course!): Be nimble and obey deadlines. This is essential for beating your competition and serving the business audience.
Excellence: The sum of the four parts—Accuracy, Brevity, Clarity and Deadlines.

You will learn the following in this chapter:

- Keys to writing excellent business stories
- How to write compelling headlines and leads
- How to write paragraphs that highlight the bigger picture

- Appropriate content to put in the rest of the story
- Important style, usage and grammar issues
- Key story-editing tips

Writing Compelling Business Stories

Once you've decided what the most pressing news is that your audience needs to know, keep your story **simple, short and sharp**.

Simple: Use easy-to-understand language, no matter whether you are writing a headline, a long narrative, a TV or radio script, a photo caption or text for a chart.

Short leads: Keep the first paragraph of a story, known as the lead, short and precise. Aim for a maximum of 25 words.

Think of writing for a radio audience. Radio scripts pack a punch and tell the listener what's important right away. **The fewer the words, the greater the readability.**

Examples:

Keepfit Inc. defaulted on its debt for the first time after talks with several hedge-fund creditors collapsed. (18 words)

Omar Rodriguez's inability to merge his airline with Flightco Inc. is a rare setback for a dealmaker whose success made him Foodland's richest man. (24 words)

Keepfit Inc. is weighing an opportunity to boost its presence in Energyland by snapping up assets from a local competitor. Its goal: to double revenue in the country.

Keepfit Inc. is considering buying the assets of a rival in Energyland to double its revenue in Businessworld's richest economy.

> Expectations that Netland will increase interest rates on Thursday couldn't be higher, but don't expect the nation's currency to benefit because any hike is already priced in, analysts said.

> Netland's currency is unlikely to gain after Thursday's expected interest rate hike because traders have already priced in the move, analysts said.

Short stories: Business readers increasingly consume news on their phones. On average, they spend fewer than 90 seconds reading narrative stories. That's between 200 and 250 words, or five or six paragraphs. For most breaking news stories, the average time spent reading is fewer than 30 seconds.

Complement short stories with visual and audio content—charts and maps, photos and tables, TV and podcasts. These all work together to provide **comprehensive coverage** to a more discerning and demanding audience with an ever-shorter attention span. The typical business reader wants to know immediately what a company, country or commodity is doing, and why.

Of course, some features and investigative stories can run several thousand words, but the **headline** and **lead** will still be the most important elements of any type of story. Unless these are instantly compelling, the reader will lose interest and move elsewhere.

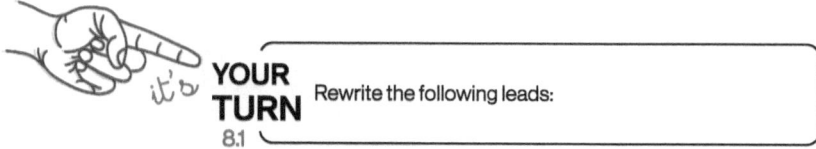

YOUR TURN 8.1 Rewrite the following leads:

After witnessing seven years of sales growth and a doubling of the company's shares, Snackable Inc.'s chief executive officer, Amelia Martin, annnounced today that she has decided to step down to head up a charitable organization next year.

As Commonland's central bank tries to assess the impact of the government's decision to raise tariffs, the hunt is back on at the central bank for hedges to protect the currency against further declines in its value.

PRO TIP

How to keep sentences short:

One thought per sentence. Don't try to explain everything in one place. Be ruthless in omitting unnecessary words.

Super Co. shares fell to their lowest in seven years after the company predicted its operating profit will decline this year and cut its dividend for the first time in a decade, giving Valuadd Inc. an opportunity to increase its market share over its closest supermarket rival.

Super Co. shares fell to a seven-year low after the supermarket chain cut its dividend for the first time in a decade and forecast lower earnings.

Solving Problems with Leads

Five quick fixes:

- Consider dividing sentences that contain a conjunction, such as "and" or "but," in two. Or rewrite.

Flightco Inc. is mired in a fare war with its main competitor that's squeezing profits, and earlier this month it cut its profit forecast for the year, blaming falling revenues at its low-cost subsidiary.

Flightco Inc.'s struggle with a fare war is squeezing profits. The carrier cut its full-year forecast this month because of falling revenue at its low-cost unit.

- Subordinate clauses are often narrative roadblocks. Consider whether such clauses could be rewritten, removed or placed lower in the story.

> **BEFORE**
> Imps Inc., Netland's second-largest telecommunications provider, is turning to the country's highest court for help with its two-year campaign to streamline operations, which it said could save it more than N$100 million annually.

> **AFTER**
> Imps Inc. is asking Netland's courts for help as the nation's second-largest telecommunications company looks to save more than N$100 million a year.

- Focus on the big-picture idea.
- In the following example, consider rewriting the lead to put the meaning of the news—the shift in tactics—up front, especially if the breaking news itself doesn't resonate with readers.

> **BEFORE**
> Energyland authorities detained four opposition leaders who helped organize protests in the nation's capital while dropping criminal charges against seven rank-and-file activists in a sign officials are shifting tactics as Prime Minister Khalil Smithe attempts to quell the biggest anti-government movement in 30 years.

> **AFTER**
> Energyland authorities are shifting tactics to quell the biggest anti-government protests in 30 years. They're arresting opposition leaders while allowing other activists to go free.

- Read the sentence aloud. If it takes more than one breath, the sentence is probably too long. Divide it in two (or three), cut superfluous words or begin again.
- Avoid word echoes. When the same word appears more than once in a paragraph, rewrite or consider a synonym. An exception is "says" and "said."
- Note in the Websville example, below, that the reporter wrote "price" three times in the first two sentences and "record" twice.

WRITING THE STORY • 153

> **BEFORE**
> Websville homes are selling for record prices as more expatriates move into the city. House prices in Netland's capital city rose 9 percent in the fourth quarter from a year earlier, according to the Websville Real Estate Association. The median transaction price was N$432,000, a new record.

> **AFTER**
> Expatriates are paying more than ever to buy homes in Websville, Netland's capital. The median sales price was a record N$432,000 in the fourth quarter, up 9 percent from a year earlier, according to the city's real estate association.

Let's examine the problems with the following lead:

Energyland President Natasha Ivanov has rejected a cabinet reshuffle announced by the prime minister, escalating a political deadlock between the former allies as the government struggles to revive an economy saddled with high inflation and a public finance crisis.

It's clear that this lead is too long and overloads the reader with too many thoughts. A good lead should explain **what** is happening and answer the question **why** or **so what**—why the reader should care. But this lead goes too far. It says **what** has happened and what this **means** (escalating a political deadlock). It then adds a **why** (the struggle to revive the economy) and the **why** behind that **why** (the inflation and public finance crisis).

The lead also assumes the president's name is well known beyond the immediate region. If it isn't, use only his or her title and put the full name lower in the story.

After:

Energyland's president escalated a feud with the prime minister by rejecting her former ally's proposed cabinet reshuffle.

Here's another lead that could benefit from a rewrite.

Shirtz Co. shares plunged the most in four years after the company warned that December sales had slipped precipitously as Netland's retail crisis spreads from bricks-and-mortar stores to e-commerce.

In this case, the lead includes all the right information. And yet the final clause—Netland's retail crisis—is arguably more important than the share-price decline. Is this perhaps the story? If so, this may be an opportunity to draw readers into the story with a single captivating idea that compels them to keep reading.
After:

Netland's retail crisis has reached the internet.

Familiar words: Use words that most English readers, listeners and viewers are likely to know. Consider the following *Before* and *After* examples:

One day after the deadline's cessation, Jones **commenced litigation.**

One day after the deadline **expired,** Jones filed a lawsuit.

The inquiry concluded that **inadequate remuneration** was the root cause of the problem.

The inquiry concluded that poor pay was the root cause of the problem.

Active verbs: Specificity is paramount in business journalism. But that doesn't mean repeating the same verbs—rose, fell, agreed to, started, ended, was, boosted, increased, and so on—in headlines and content. Be bold in your word choices, without exaggerating. Vigorous verbs make headlines and sentences sing.

Energyland Missile Strike Escalates Tensions With Supplyland

Veggi Shares Plunge as Revenue Forecast Misses All Analyst Estimates

Agriculture Slump Drags Foodland Closer to Recession

Nationwide Protests Erupt in Energyland

Netland Markets Surge as Driverless Wins Contract Deal With Union

Active sentences: An active sentence focuses on the "doer," which in business is usually a person, company, country, government, institution or security. A currency strengthens. A commodity falls. A business leader quits. A company expands. A stock plummets. In a passive sentence, an action is done to the subject.

Active:

In Energyland, the Department of Natural Resources **regulates** wind farms.

Passive:

In Energyland, wind farms **are regulated by** the Department of Natural Resources.

Traditional retailers like Auld Inc. are getting squeezed by discounters Bargin Co. and Cheap Inc. while more people are buying groceries online from home.

Discount retailers Bargin Co. and Cheap Inc. are squeezing traditional grocers like Auld Inc. as more people shop online.

An exception to using the active voice is when the writer needs to focus on the protagonist. In the example below, the company whose credit rating is being cut is more important than the ratings agency that is taking the action.

Ratings Agency Cuts Veggi's Investment-Grade Rating After Profit Warning

Veggi Rating Cut to Non-Investment Grade by Ratings Agency After Profit Warning

Rewrite the following sentence:

Build Co., the nation's largest constructor, is set to commence the refurbishment of 10,000 state-owned family dwellings after finalizing a C$400 million agreement with the Commmonland government to upgrade the accomodation, the company announced.

Superlatives: Find and use superlatives to write compelling business stories. They offer the context and surprise that readers, listeners and viewers need to understand the news and to take action. It's more useful to write that oil fell to its lowest price in three years than to say oil prices declined 2 percent.

Superlatives such as biggest, smallest, longest, shortest, highest, lowest, fastest or slowest add color and depth to stories about companies, countries and assets.

Examples:

- The currency fell to a **seven-week low**.
- The shares rose to a **record**.

- XYZ's chocolate sales topped ABC's for the **first time in four years**.
- Oil suffered its **biggest decline in three months**.
- The economy grew at its **fastest pace in 11 quarters**.

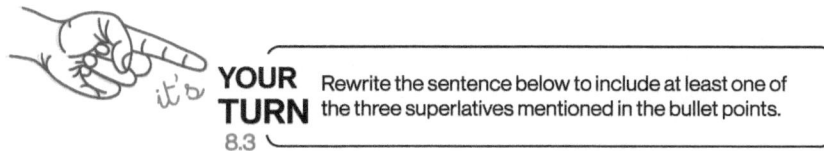

YOUR TURN 8.3 Rewrite the sentence below to include at least one of the three superlatives mentioned in the bullet points.

Robo Corp. is poised to re-enter Netland's bond market this week with a N$800 million offering that will help to fund at least 150 new warehouses.

- It's the first time in three years that Robo Corp. will issue bonds in Netland.
- The N$800 million bond will be its largest ever.
- The 150 new warehouses will double the company's warehouse capacity.

Precision: Specificity is a key to excellence in business writing. Let's look at one sentence:

Keepfit enjoyed double-digit growth in the last year.

At first glance, the sentence appears intelligible. It's not. Every word, apart from the company name, can be questioned.

- "Enjoyed" is imprecise and subjective. It assumes that double-digit growth is a positive outcome for Keepfit. But it could be that Keepfit sales grew 10 percent while the company had forecast 20 percent growth.
- "Double-digit" is imprecise. It can mean anything from 10 percent to 99 percent. It's also financial jargon, which analysts (and journalists) sometimes spout because it sounds authoritative. Remember that if you don't understand what's being said or written, it's likely your audience won't either.
- "Growth" lacks precision unless the reader knows what kind of growth. Of revenue? Of profit? Of the number of units produced or sold?
- "In the last year" could be interpreted as the past 52 weeks, the last calendar year, the last business (fiscal) year, or the year so far.

Some possible rewrites, depending on the context:

Keepfit shares rose 28 percent last year.
Keepfit revenue gained 43 percent last year.
Keepfit net income increased 10 percent last year.
Keepfit opened 23 percent more gyms last year.
Keepfit sold 45 percent more athletic equipment in the past 12 months.

Imprecise:

Sales of electric vehicles were *a fraction of* total deliveries.

Specific:

Sales of electric vehicles were *less than 8 percent* of total deliveries.

Imprecise:

The introduction of a *low* value-added tax on consumer goods in March stoked inflation, economists said.

Specific:

The introduction of a *2 percent* value-added tax on consumer goods in March stoked inflation, economists said.

Headlines

Every word in a headline is critical. Every headline should be illuminating, interesting and immediately understandable. The best ones convey a combination of the following: News of the moment, a surprise, names of prominent companies and/or people, conflict, drama and superlatives.

Headlines are written in many different ways, depending on the intended audience.

Traders, for example, want short, straightforward headlines that only give them essential **market-moving** news. They rely on such headlines, often called **flash headlines**, to quickly buy or sell shares, bonds, currencies or commodities.

Investors and money managers want to know what happened, why, where, when and the source. They don't want fluff or hype. They want to make money. They want the news and its meaning in as few words as possible.

Seconds count. Flash headlines are usually written in the present tense and in a shorthand that investors understand.

Example:

NETLAND 2Q GDP EXPANDS 1.9 PERCENT Q/Q; EST. 1.7 PERCENT

The above flash headline means that Netland's gross domestic product increased 1.9 percent in the second quarter (2Q; i.e., April–June) versus the previous quarter (1Q; i.e., January–March). The median estimate (Est.) of economists was for 1.7 percent growth, according to data compiled by the *Netland Post*.

In other words, the headline shows traders that Netland's economy has been growing faster than economists' projections. That may prompt them to buy Netland's currency and shares in its leading companies and to sell its sovereign bonds.

Story headlines, in contrast to flash headlines, are designed for a more general audience. Some simply tell the reader what has happened.

Bankland Chooses Nigel Easterbrook to Head Transportation Ministry

Foodland President Calls for Inquiry Into Financial Misconduct

Most story headlines go beyond the **what** (figure 8.1). They add value, such as a superlative or basic context. They often explain **why** something has happened or tell the reader **what the news means**, also known as the *so what*. They are usually written in the present tense.

One rule of thumb: **Don't begin writing a story without a headline in mind.** Assuming the reporting is complete, it's good discipline to write a possible headline, keeping in mind that it may change as the story develops. If the headline doesn't inspire, it may be a sign that the story needs additional reporting or reframing.

WHAT + ADDED VALUE

Netland Home Prices Post First Annual Increase in Four Years
Wallgen Bank Sells Online Stake to OneBank, Raising $400 Million

WHAT + WHY

Growth Asset Traders to Leave After Fund Posts Loss in November
Eatmore Plunges After Restaurant Chain's CEO, CFO Resign

WHAT + MEANING

Bank of Netland Deposits Jump in Sign It's Intervening to Curb Currency Slide
ValuAdd Decline Underscores Hurdles Facing CEO Turnaround Plan

Other business-story headlines, particularly those written for features and the web, are designed to grab readers' attention.

ATTENTION-GRABBING

Long Before Crash, Flightco Pilot Warned Bosses of Dangers
Keepfit Chief Explains Why He Wants to Kill the Business He Founded

FIGURE 8.1 What plus.

How to Write a Headline

The headline's theme should be understandable immediately. If not, rewrite. In the following example, the theme of the story—the Netland dollar—isn't mentioned until the sixth and seventh words. That's too late. The busy trader scanning multiple headlines wants to know the news right away.

No Cheer in Sight for Netland Dollar Amid Political, Trade Discord

Netland Dollar Seen Tumbling More Amid Trade, Political Discord

Headlines written for an online audience often need to be simpler and more compelling because the readership is broader and less financially knowledgeable.

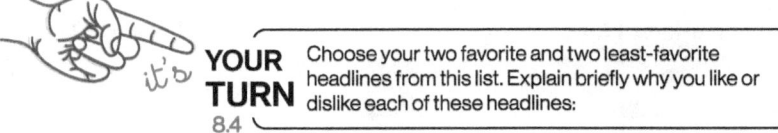

YOUR TURN 8.4 Choose your two favorite and two least-favorite headlines from this list. Explain briefly why you like or dislike each of these headlines:

Ex-ABC Trader Says He Was Trained to Lie to Customers

The Most Mind-Numbing of Office Tasks Made One Man a Billionaire

Economist Sees Goldilocks Economy Next Year Barring Zombie Apocalypse

Nicki Zhang Runs 50 Kilometers Daily. Now She Wants to Run Your Country

Will They Help, Hurt or Do Nothing? Central Banks Face Uncertainty

ChemPet's New Factory Means Prosperity for One Town, Disaster for Another

Avoid:

- Cluttering headlines with unnecessary numbers, attribution and time references. Instead, add percentages and include a why.

Flightco Profit Rises to F$2.65 Billion From F$2.37 Billion, Company Says

Flightco Profit Rises 12% as Record Holiday Sales Inflate Margins

- Headlines that state the obvious:

  Climate Change Seen Making Netland Hotter This Summer

  Commonland Shoppers Still Want Bargains This Holiday Season

- Alphabet soup:

  Netland FCA to Review BGC Pre-Bid Stake Purchase in AI

- Unfamiliar abbreviations or acronyms:

Commission Tells Netland to Adopt **AML** Rule or Face Court

Commission Orders Netland to Adopt Anti-Money Laundering **Rule**

- Unfamiliar names of companies or people:

Commonland Currency Plunges on Report **Burford's** Airplane Is Missing

Commonland Currency Plunges on Report Finance Minister's Plane Is Missing

- Puns, cliches, jargon and alliteration:

    Quest for Zest Gets Tough for Fragrance Firm Following Fire

    Airline in Turbulence, Headed for Rough Landing Unless Financing Found

    WTI Dips Below 50-Day MA as Brent Settles in Lower Boll. Band

    Madhouse Market for Money Managers Makes Martin Miserable

- An excess of label headlines that begin with words and phrases such as "What," "How," "This," "Meet The," and "Here Are The Top Five/10 . . . "

Let's look at some pairs of headlines to see why the rewrite is more compelling than the original.

Inject's Hacking Mess Is Setback to New CEO's Turnaround Plan

New Inject Chief's Hacking Nightmare Is Latest in String of Setbacks

The original headline lacks drama. Unless readers are interested specifically in Inject Inc., they're unlikely to click on the story. The rewrite is a **surprise** and appeals to a **broader audience**.

> Netland Currency Bears Back Off as Record New Year Rally Suggests Bounce

> Netland Currency Has Strongest-Ever Start to a Year as Economy Grows

The original headline is difficult to absorb in one reading. The rewrite is **simple**, and the **superlative**—strongest-ever—draws readers' attention.

> Prime Minister Misfires Message Containing Cell Phone Number

> Prime Minister Accidentally Sends Her Phone Number to 16 Million Followers

The original headline, while accurate, isn't conversational or catchy. The magnitude of the error doesn't stand out. In the rewrite, the nugget of data—16 million followers—tells the story perfectly.

Foodland Internet CEO Becomes Billionaire on Remote Work Boom

Remote Work Boom Mints Another Internet Billionaire

The rewritten headline is more appealing because it focuses on remote work rather than on one CEO in one Businessworld country.

YOUR TURN 8.5 Read the following leads and write a headline of no more than 12 words for each:

> Bankland's inflation rate, the lowest in more than five years, will probably accelerate to 6.7% by the end of the year, Growth Asset Management told investors in a weekly note.

> Sip Corp. has agreed to sell its sugar-refining business in Supplyland to Sweeti Inc. as concern about obesity and diabetes leads to declines in consumption.

> Energyland's government will double its spending on roads, bridges, electricity and clean water in remote areas next year, Prime Minister Khalil Smithe said in a speech today in Gasopolis.

How to Write a Lead

The lead sets the tone for your business story. It should inform, educate and surprise. It often offers insight and perspective, conflict and tension. It's the hook—the paragraph that draws in your audience, usually by telling them something they need to know, unfettered by excess words, numbers or jargon (figure 8.2).

Thinking Like an Editor

Here's one editor's thought process after reading a story submitted by her economics reporter. Here's her lead:

Foodland economic growth accelerated in the third quarter to 2.9% after an uninspiring first half of the year as a build-up of inventories and a soybean-related jump in exports helped cushion softer household spending. (35 words)

> "Not bad, but too long. It should be more snappy and digestible. Time's pressing. The easiest step is to remove the backward-looking phrase 'after an uninspiring first half of the year.'"

Foodland economic growth accelerated in the third quarter to 2.9% as a build-up of inventories and a soybean-related jump in exports helped cushion softer household spending. (27 words)

> "Still too long. Hmm, do I need to mention 2.9% growth? That number was in the flash headline and in the initial bullet-point story fill. Let's put it in the second paragraph. Let's change 'a build-up of inventories' to 'rising inventories' and 'a soybean-related jump in exports' to 'increased soybean exports.' That makes the lead more palatable."

Foodland economic growth accelerated in the third quarter as rising inventories and increased soybean exports helped cushion softer household spending. (20 words)

> "OK, it works but still feels bland. Why soybeans? Two ideas. Stick with the lead and write a shorter sidebar about soybeans. Or focus on soybeans in the lead and add information about Foodland economic growth in the second paragraph. Let's see what the reporter and another editor think."

Soybeans helped power Foodland's economy last quarter after exports of the protein-rich legume doubled. (15 words)

> "The lead is stronger now. And 'last quarter' works better than 'in the third quarter.' Let's publish!"

FIGURE 8.2 Thinking like an editor.

There are many ways to write a lead, depending on the point of the story and the intended audience. Some contain all the relevant details that a time-strapped reader needs. Others pull in the reader with an alluring image that prods the individual to move from one paragraph to the next as the story line is gracefully revealed.

Never forget that **you are a storyteller**, taking your readers on a journey that begins with a compelling theme. Unless readers are drawn into the story immediately, they won't feel inclined to read the prose beneath.

Good leads have:

- A sense of direction. Business news is usually positive or negative. It's up or down, rarely sideways. In a story where the news is nuanced, start with the most compelling argument and mention alternatives lower down.

Netland productivity fell unexpectedly for the first time in 18 months, calling into question the strength of the economy after five years of growth.

Energyland is on track to lure E$100 billion in new investment over the next five years, with more than half already committed, President Natasha Ivanov said Tuesday.

- A clear theme.

Bankland's state pension board said it has invested more than B$10 billion in solar power projects the past year while dumping its oil holdings to embrace the rush to renewable energy.

- Tension or surprise.

This is what passes for good news in Energyland these days: The country's four-year economic deceleration appears to have stabilized.

- A what and a why.

Supplyland's currency rose 0.7 percent after industrial production had its biggest gain in a year.

Chip Co. shares plunged after the company disclosed that Supplyland authorities have been probing its accounting practices for more than a year.

- A what and a so-what.

Screenplex Corp.'s market share in Netland fell for the first time in eight months in June, a setback to its ambition to overtake Cinema Inc. as the country's largest movie-theater company.

- Attribution.
- Not all stories require attribution in the lead if it's clear where the news came from. But all stories must be transparent. The reader, listener or viewer needs to know the source of the information. When attribution is required, it's better to put it at the end of the sentence unless the person named is significant enough to merit leading with his or her name.

> Zdenek Jetlinek, ChemPet Inc.'s deputy chief executive officer, said Wednesday that the petrochemicals company is considering a bid for a stake in Energyland's oil pipeline network.

> ChemPet Inc. may bid for a stake in Energyland's oil pipeline network, the company's deputy chief executive officer said Wednesday.

- Rhythm.
- When done well, two-sentence leads can be dynamic. Think of the second sentence as a punchline, which is usually shorter than the first.

The floods that devastated northern Supplyland last month left Peasplus Corp.'s wheat fields mostly unscathed. Draining them is still going to cost a fortune.

It boasts a gym, pool, bowling alley and helipad—not to mention rooms for 28 guests—and it's for sale for half its original price. So why can't billionaire Nick Yamamoto find a buyer for his superyacht?

- Unexpected twists.
The following leads grab attention because they're counter-intuitive and surprising.

In Bankland's equity market, the worse a company's finances, the better its stock does.

For a company that no longer makes televisions, Robo Corp. still makes a lot of money from this twentieth-century analog technology.

- Momentum.
- A good lead takes the story forward without dwelling on history or background. That momentum should extend into the second paragraph.
- Notice in the following example how the momentum of the lead slows because of the backward-looking phrase "after a series of major disposals." By removing those words, the reader can see the point of the story more quickly. The focus of the rewrite depends on whether the story is about the cash pile, the CEO or the company.

Sweeti Inc.'s cash pile swelled to $17.5 billion in the third quarter after a series of major disposals, and investors want to know what Chief Executive Officer Ivan Murphy will do with it.

Sweeti Inc.'s cash pile swelled to $17.5 billion last quarter, and investors want to know what Chief Executive Officer Ivan Murphy will do with it.

- Consistency.

  Story headlines and leads should be consistent. A straight-news lead shouldn't necessarily mimic or use the same language as the headline, but the theme and focus should be similar.

  Foodland Investor Sentiment Improves as Central Bank Acts

  Investor confidence in Foodland's economic outlook rose from an eight-year low after the nation's central bank stepped up monetary stimulus and geopolitical tensions eased.

Rewrite the following headline and lead so that they're consistent:

Linen's 'Fluffy' Cushion Sales Drop 20% as Furnishing Fad Fades

Linen Co. shares had their biggest drop in two years after Supplyland's largest textile maker said it sold 200 million items of top-selling 'Fluffy' cushions last year, down from a record 250 million a year earlier, as a fad for its branded soft-furnishings faded. The shares fell 11% to S$44.

The Second Paragraph: Maintain the Momentum

The **momentum** of the lead should continue into the **second paragraph** and beyond. Too often, the second paragraph becomes a dumping ground for details, numbers or history and ends up interrupting the flow of the narrative rather than helping it along.

It's important to focus on what is new and gradually weave in context and history to keep the reader's attention from drifting.

YOUR TURN it's **8.7** — Read the lead below.

> Eatmore Co. indefinitely postponed plans to open 150 steak restaurants across Energyland after vegan activists vowed to prevent customers from entering the eateries.
>
> In your own words, write three or four big-picture sentences in a bullet-point format based on the information below. Then, write one big-picture paragraph that gives insight into the breaking news.
>
> > The shares fell 14% to C$27.50, the largest percentage decline in five years. Four of 14 analysts who follow the company downgraded the stock. The analysts' 12-month average target price for Eatmore fell to C$22, 20% below today's closing price.
> >
> > The postponement is an embarrassment for Kenji Hargreaves, Eatmore's chief executive officer for the past four years, who was born and raised in Energyland. Hargreaves, 47, moved to Commonland after finishing graduate school 23 years ago. Hargreaves, who is divorced, is an avid skier. Hargreaves has long been friendly with Natasha Ivanov, Energyland's president. Ivanov is vegan.
> >
> > The postponement appears to stymie Eatmore's plans to open more restaurants outside Commonland, where it has 174 company-owned outlets and 170 franchises. Eatmore also has 47 restaurants in Netland.
> >
> > The decision will give a fillip to Mysteak Inc., a privately-owned chain of restaurants in Energyland, and to Steak N Chips Co., which announced plans last year to open restaurants in Energyland. Steak N Chips is based in Netland, where it has 470 restaurants. The company's shares rose 4% today.

How to Write a Big-Picture Paragraph

Business journalists are under increasing pressure to go beyond the breaking story as quickly as possible. Readers, viewers and listeners now demand **instant authoritative analysis**. Merely saying what happened isn't enough.

Every story is an opportunity to provide **relative value**—context and comparison—that makes news from one place relevant and understandable elsewhere. The same applies to stories about companies and markets. Traders, investors and executives always consider relative value when deciding what to buy, sell or take action on.

This context is often contained in a "big-picture" paragraph that tells readers **what's at stake**, **why they should care** about the story and **why the story is significant now**. Different news organizations call the big-picture paragraph by different names, including "key insights," "instant insights," "nut paragraphs" and "cosmic paragraphs."

Big-picture paragraphs aren't reams of facts, but rather an attempt to zoom out of the immediate development and show how the news fits into a broader trend. They try to synthesize **what the news means** to investors, countries, companies and people.

These insights can be woven into a story at any place. They are often found near the top of the story to help the reader understand why the news is important. They can even be part of the lead or placed directly after the lead to give context. Longer stories often have two or three big-picture paragraphs scattered throughout the narrative, depending on the structure and theme.

Big-picture paragraphs work best when reporters know their beats intimately and when they can write authoritatively about such questions as:

- Why is today's news significant?
- How will it change the company's or country's fortunes?
- Who are the winners and losers?

As much as possible, these sentences should be forward-looking and avoid regurgitating background information that's already public.

The following words and phrases are frequently found in big-picture paragraphs:

The latest event, announcement or story twist **signals, illustrates, suggests, means, shows, highlights, reflects, epitomizes, underscores, underpins, complicates efforts to, poses a threat to, is evidence that, throws a spotlight on, dramatizes the need for, mirrors, represents a challenge to, complements, is further proof that, is the clearest indication that.**

Big-picture paragraphs often begin with phrases such as: **At stake is; At the heart of the debate/discussion/issue is; Hanging in the balance is.**

These are **language prompts** to help the writer step back from the narrow focus of a story and give it wider context. The more that a writer can weave such insights about economic, political and market developments into stories, the better.

In the same way that a cartoonist tries to capture the essence of a story in a drawing, a writer should try to capture the spirit or heart of the narrative in one clear paragraph. Big-picture paragraphs often convey

- **Images**, rather than facts
- The **impact** of the news, rather than historical information
- The **importance** of the news to a broad audience

Examples:

For Investing Inc., the takeover **marks the biggest expansion** into commercial banking yet under Alison Bautista, who became chief executive officer in December and promised to end five years of losses.

The move **highlights** the dilemma of Energyland's government. If it implements democratic reforms, it may lose the election. If it doesn't, the government faces the very real threat of an uprising among citizens frustrated by higher prices and fewer jobs.

The board's **decision is** an embarrassment for Sweeti Chief Executive Officer Ivan Murphy, who spent months championing his deputies' efforts to explore new businesses only to have the plan overturned by the directors.

The dispute **illustrates** the intensifying clash over biofuel policy that's pitting two political constituencies—farmers and energy companies—against each other.

Quotations

During every interview, conference call and press conference, a good business reporter should be considering—and making a note of—which quotes to use in the story and where they fit into the narrative.

Quotations should breathe life into a story, not just repeat facts or jargon. They should be used strategically to help advance the story rather than being thrown in for the sake of it.

Never—repeat, never—change a quote or add words that a person has not said.

PRO TIP

Nine keys to using quotations in stories:

1. The first quote should ratify the story's theme and make the reader **eager** to move on.
2. **Short quotes** typically have greater impact. Long, explanatory quotes rarely work.
3. **Avoid cliches and jargon**, even when people use them.
4. **Remove throat-clearing** at the start of a quote such as "In my opinion…"
5. Don't put **quote marks** around mere assertions of fact. Quote marks signify you are adding something more than a fact — an opinion, a prediction, a unique analysis, an emotion.
6. **Avoid** quotes that simply **repeat** the news.
7. Quotes should sound like a **human being speaking**, even if they have been taken from a press release.
8. Quote people with the most **at stake.**
9. Let the reader know why the person quoted is **credible.** For example, quote the economist who correctly predicted a central-bank decision, the analyst whose recommendation for a stock was the most accurate, the manager of a top-performing bond fund. This gives the story authority

Many long-form narratives have a **kicker quote** at the very end of the story. These bring closure to the article, often offering a surprise, revelation or image that lingers with the reader.

Here are two examples of kicker quotes that an accomplished reporter showed to the interns.

For a story on accidents by autonomous vehicles:

"The biggest public-relations nightmares are ahead," Johnston said. "There's only one way to the goal. Through the minefield."

For a story on private equity companies:

"Economic innovation is the driving force of the economy, but you would hope that people who get run over are helped," Chan said.

YOUR TURN 8.8 The quotation below is just a series of facts. Rewrite the sentence, and highlight the most important or compelling partial or full quote.

"By year's end, we expect to be cultivating 50,000 hectares, and we will be producing 50,000 tons of palm oil a year within three years," Peasplus Chief Executive Officer Angela Singh said in a phone interview. "By then, we should be making a hefty profit from the product."

Which of the following quotations, if any, are suitable for use in stories?

"The board fully appreciates the support that is being received from all stakeholders and the commitment that is being shown," a spokesman said.

"The major concern for most corporates as well as potential investors last year was the election and the possible implications for policy direction, especially from an exchange-rate perspective," Jamie Johnson, Auld Inc.'s chief financial officer, said.

"The board has approved the structure of the proposed recapitalization plan," a spokesman said.

Rewrite the following quotation in the form of a lead.

"We are having fruitful discussions with prospective partners right now," Snackable spokesman Nicky Chen said. "It's what we're doing this week. We're hoping to conclude a deal by the end of the month if all goes well."

The Rest of the Story

The first 200 words of most breaking-news business stories—four or five paragraphs—should contain all the key details and insights that a reader needs to know. It takes the average reader about 90 seconds to read 200 words.

For major breaking news and updates to already published stories, consider adding the following:

- **Secondary big-picture paragraphs** that explore different angles to the story's theme.
- **Bullet points** for details that back up the narrative. These work well when there are a lot of numbers or hard-to-read names of individuals or companies.
- A **to-be-sure paragraph** containing arguments that may counter the story's main theme or highlight an alternate trend.
- A **forward spin** to explain what might happen next.
- **Comparisons** with other people, companies, economies, countries or regions. Is the trend or theme the exception or the rule?
- More **history** or **context**, with links to related stories.
- Additional **multimedia** content, including links to TV, social media or radio clips, podcasts and explanatory stories.
- **More quotations** from experts and people involved in the story that shed light on different aspects of the narrative.
- **More anecdotes, data and other details that back up the theme.** This evidence can appear wherever appropriate.

The additional elements will vary depending on whether the story is breaking news or a longer piece of analytical enterprise.

The Final Word

Good writing matters, regardless of the format in which it's presented and regardless of the platform on which it appears. Headlines and leads are the principal battleground because they're what most readers and viewers see and hear. Yet when telling the business story, every noun, verb, sentence, chart, illustration and argument carries weight. For more on awkward words and phrases, jargon, cliches, hype, numbers, and commonly used (and abused) style in business journalism, see Words to Watch in Appendix 1.

Working together, reporters and editors must ensure that the story's structure is appropriate. The lead should be clearly articulated. The narrative should tell readers why the story is important and keep them interested. Big-picture themes should be highlighted.

When a business story is clear, focused and insightful, it has the potential to reach and influence a huge and diverse audience of investors, policy makers, business leaders and other readers.

9

Data and Visuals

The First Word

High-speed computing and the growth of the internet have led to an explosion of publicly available data. Yet while an increasing number of journalists have computer-science knowledge and use Microsoft Excel spreadsheets with ease, others are intimidated or overwhelmed by what they perceive as the complexities of computer-assisted reporting and data-driven journalism.

Not all business journalists desire to become number-crunching experts, of course. But it's critical to know the basics of quantitative literacy—how to evaluate survey results, an understanding of simple mathematical formulas, for example—and to ask questions with a critical eye when the meaning of the data is unclear.

Journalists also need another skill—the ability to present data so that the business audience grasps their significance immediately. Is the best way to tell the story through words, charts, tables, infographics, a timeline, audio, video, some other visual format, or a mixture? This chapter addresses this and other fundamental decisions about working with data and visual information.

You will learn the following in this chapter:

- Numeracy skills for business journalists
- Data-story categories
- Best practices for working with data sets
- Best practices for charts and graphs
- Tips for improving charts

Numeracy Skills

Calculate Percentage Change

In business journalism, the percentage change between two numbers is usually more important than the numbers themselves.

Memorize this percentage-change formula: **(A − B)/B × 100**.

Let's say you're trying to calculate how much **larger** one number is than another. In this case, if A is 150 and B is 90, 150 minus 90 = 60. Now divide 60 by 90 and multiply by 100 = 67%.

(150 − 90)/90 × 100 = 67%.

In other words, **A is 67 percent larger than B**.

Conversely, if you want to know by what percentage B is **smaller** than A, the formula is: **(B − A)/A × 100**.

(90 − 150)/150 × 100 = 40%.

In other words, **B is 40 percent smaller than A**.

In stories, lead with the percentage change unless the numbers themselves are more relevant. Add the actual numbers lower in the story if such details are necessary.

BEFORE

Brie Inc. fell to F$20.20 from F$20.93 yesterday, pulling down Foodland's benchmark index after the cheesemaker reported a 7% decline in second-half sales.

Brie Inc. fell 3.5% after the cheesemaker reported a decline in second-half sales.

AFTER

it's YOUR TURN Rewrite the following leads:

9.1

Bankland home prices fell in October to an average of B$304,770 from B$307,600 a month earlier, Houseprice Inc. said in a report Tuesday. It was the seventh successive month-on-month decline.

Inject Inc. profit amounted to C$659.6 million last year compared with C$439.9 million a year earlier, after Commonand's largest pharmaceuticals company introduced its first lung-cancer drug, Lungiarte, which generated more than C$5 billion in sales.

BEFORE

The airline's net income fell to E$900 million in the 12 months ended Dec. 31. That compared with a profit of E$1 billion the previous year.

Net income fell 10% to E$900 million last year.

AFTER

Calculate Earnings per Share

Earnings per share (EPS)—net income divided by the number of outstanding shares—is a widely watched measure for estimating a company's performance against itself over time and against its rivals. It shows how much profit a company generates for each share. EPS usually excludes extraordinary items and discontinued operations. It's usually viewed on a diluted basis.

If net income is E$1 million and there are 500,000 outstanding shares, the EPS is E$2. If net income is E$5.5 million and there are 10 million shares outstanding, the EPS is E$0.55.

Use Numbers Sparingly

Too many numbers can make the eyes glaze over. One number—or no numbers—in a lead is usually sufficient. Add numbers sparingly or choose a different format, such as a chart or a table, to display them.

Build Co. profit rose a greater-than-expected 28% to $309.4 million in the third quarter as revenue gained 17%, topping $4 billion for the first time as construction contracts surged.

Build Co. profit rose more than expected in the third quarter as construction contracts surged.

BEFORE

> The global stock of negative-yielding debt topped E$17 trillion this week as this year's unprecedented bond rally notched up yet another 13-digit milestone amid rising market volatility.

AFTER

> The global supply of negative-yielding debt topped a record E$17 trillion this week as rising market volatility lends extra force to this year's unprecedented bond rally.

In the example above, the writer doesn't explain the significance of the E$17 trillion figure and tries too hard to be creative by mentioning the "13-digit milestone."

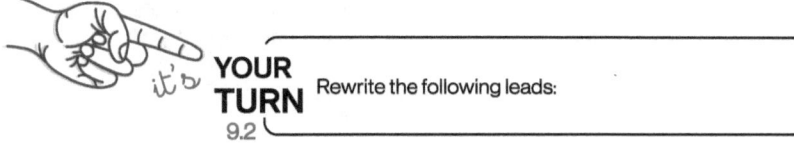

YOUR TURN 9.2 Rewrite the following leads:

> Auld Inc. shares fell 4.7% to close at S$21.51 after declining to a one-year intraday low of S$20.73 following the unexpected resignation of Chief Financial Officer Jamie Johnson.

> Supplyland's trade deficit rose to a record S$214 billion in August from S$204 billion a month earlier and S$196 billion a year earlier after an 8% surge in oil imports and a 27% decline in exports of electronic products.

> Cocoa gained for a third day, jumping as much as 5.8% to the highest level in more than two years, after Foodland acknowledged earlier reports that an unknown disease was blighting the crop in two key growing regions.

Make Numbers Come Alive

Comparisons with familiar concepts, places and objects help bring dry numbers to life.

> The football-field-sized warehouse contains more than 700,000 pairs of sneakers.
> Lifting the ban would create 4.4 billion tons of carbon emissions, the equivalent of running 42 coal plants for a lifetime.

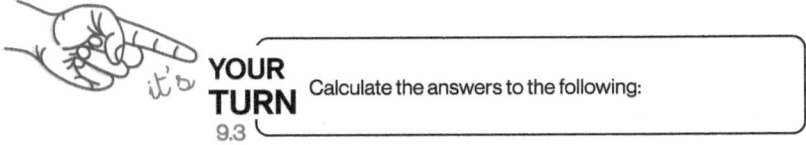

YOUR TURN 9.3 Calculate the answers to the following:

A power plant produces 200 megawatts of electricity per year in an area where the average home uses 5,000 watts annually. How many homes can the power plant supply per year? (1 megawatt = 1 million watts)

Wear Inc.'s new factory is 200 meters long and 120 meters wide. That's the equivalent of how many soccer pitches? (Assume that a standard soccer pitch is 105 meters long and 68 meters wide.)

Sip Corp. produces 10 million cases of beer a year, in cases of 12 half-liter bottles. That's enough to fill how many Olympic-size swimming pools? (Assume that an Olympic pool is 50 meters long, 25 meters wide and 2 meters deep. There are 1,000 liters in a cubic meter.)

Imps Inc. sold 231.2 million phones last year and 211.9 million the year before. If the phones for both years were laid end to end, how many times would they circle the Earth? (Assume that an average phone is 140 millimeters long, and the Earth's circumference is about 40,000 kilometers.)

Mean, Median and Mode: The Differences

The mean. This is the average of a group of numbers. Add the values and divide the total by the number of values.

For example, you want to know the **average** of five numbers: 7, 12, 14, 19 and 23. Their total is 75. Divide 75 by 5 = 15. That's the average or mean. This is used most for calculations, especially for earnings estimates.

The median. This is the middle number in a group of figures. In the group of five numbers above, the **middle number** is 14. The median is often used when a data set has outliers that might skew the result. For example, in the following data set—5, 7, 12, 14, 19, 23 and 247—the last number is an outlier so the median is more helpful to the reader than the average. Business journalists often use the median number when looking at economic data estimates, such as GDP or CPI.

The mode. This is the value that occurs **most often** in a data set. For example, in the following group of numbers—28, 72, 72, 93, 111—the mode is 72 because it appears twice. The mode is rarely used.

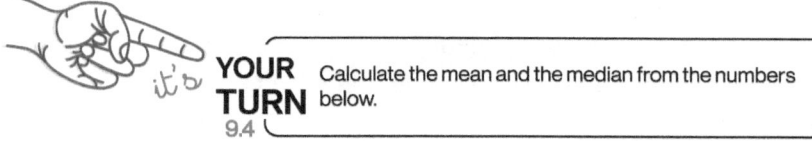

YOUR TURN 9.4 Calculate the mean and the median from the numbers below.

Seven analysts gave estimates of Hospit Inc.'s fourth-quarter net income. They were: C$137 million, C$142 million, C$116 million, C$184 million, C$155 million, C$136 million and C$173 million.
What was the mean estimate?

Seven economists gave forecasts for Supplyland's October trade balance. They were: S$137 billion, S$142 billion, S$116 billion, S$184 billion, S$155 billion, S$136 billion and S$173 billion.
What was the median figure?

Using Data Sets

Before analyzing what any data set means, it's imperative to examine how the numbers appear on spreadsheets and to consider what may be missing or what may skew the findings.

That's because large sets of numbers are often **incomplete** or **imperfect**. Further, data can be **manipulated, mismanaged** or **misused**, either unintentionally or deliberately. To avoid coming to errant conclusions, Sandeep Junnarkar, a professor of interactive journalism at City University of New York, suggests that students look out for the following when using Excel spreadsheets:

- Duplicate numbers
- Dates written incorrectly
- Inconsistent names, formats and units
- Unclear terms, codes and abbreviations
- Numbers appearing as text and vice versa
- Extra spaces
- Empty cells

Most of these inconsistencies and errors can be fixed using basic Excel commands and formulas.

But increasingly, Excel isn't enough for analyzing information with tens of thousands, or even millions, of data points. That's why coding has become a valued skill in newsrooms, especially newsrooms reporting on business and finance. Computer programs written by data journalists are often used to scrape websites for data, clean up inconsistencies and analyze the information in a time frame that would be impossible for a human to do.

Charts and Graphics

After analyzing the data, the next question is how best to display the findings. Readers and viewers remember unusual or unexpected visualization types and graphics more than basic graphs and charts. But there often isn't time or necessity to go beyond the tried and tested.

Let's examine a few basic chart types, keeping in mind that the reader or viewer needs to be able to understand what the chart means almost instantly. **Each chart should stand alone** and not rely on an accompanying article to convey the meaning.

Bar charts are usually used for comparing specific and discrete values, such as the number of wind farms or the unemployment rate in each Businessworld country.

Most common are **vertical** bar charts. For example, the x axis across the bottom of the chart would show compensation ranges (below $20,000, $20,001–$40,000, $40,001–60,000 and so on), and the y axis would show the number or percentage of people earning these amounts. Bar charts always start at zero.

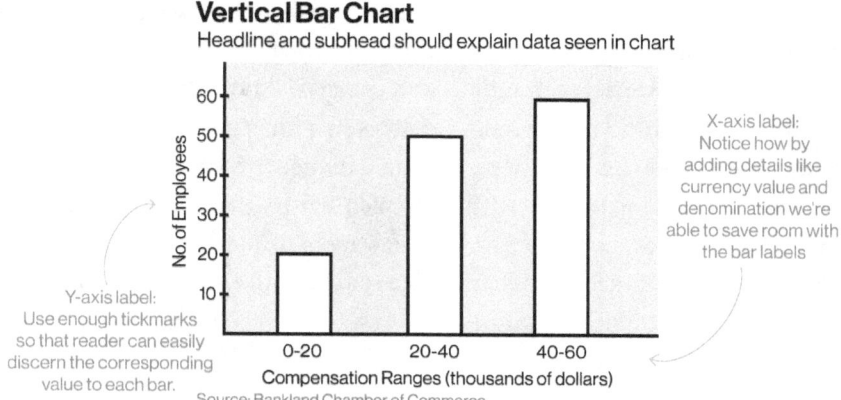

FIGURE 9.1 Vertical bar chart.

Horizontal bar charts are useful when arranging variables in lists. For example, a chart could illustrate the number of stores in different countries, with the largest number at the top ranging to the smallest at the bottom.

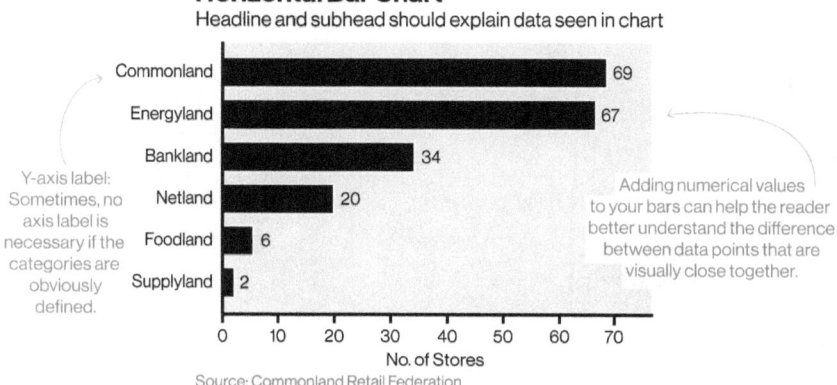

FIGURE 9.2 Horizontal bar chart.

Line charts are usually used to display connected values over time. A basic line chart could show, for example, the price of a stock over the past year. The x axis shows each month and the y axis shows the price.

When comparing two or more variables in a line chart, it's best to have only one y axis. This usually means the data need to be **normalized** so that one can compare like with like, such as the percentage change in several stock prices over the past year. Beware of displaying too many variables, which risks turning a chart into a spaghetti-like jumble.

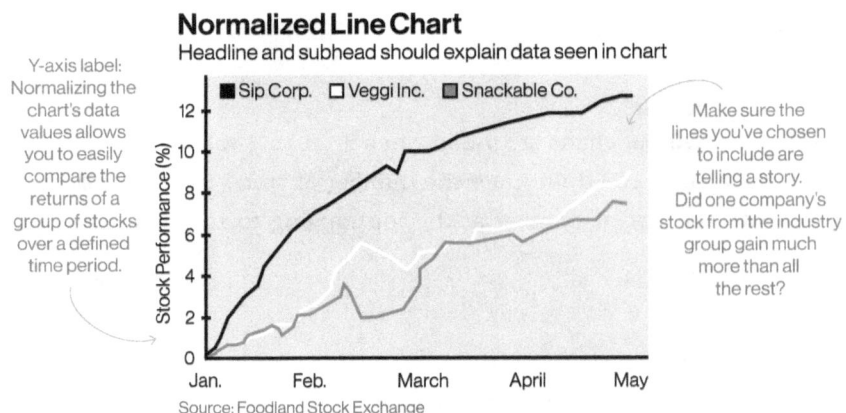

FIGURE 9.3 Normalized line chart.

Pie charts can only show component parts of a whole; that is, the proportion of sales from one country versus others. They're not useful when the proportions are tiny.

Pie Chart
Headline and subhead should explain data seen in chart

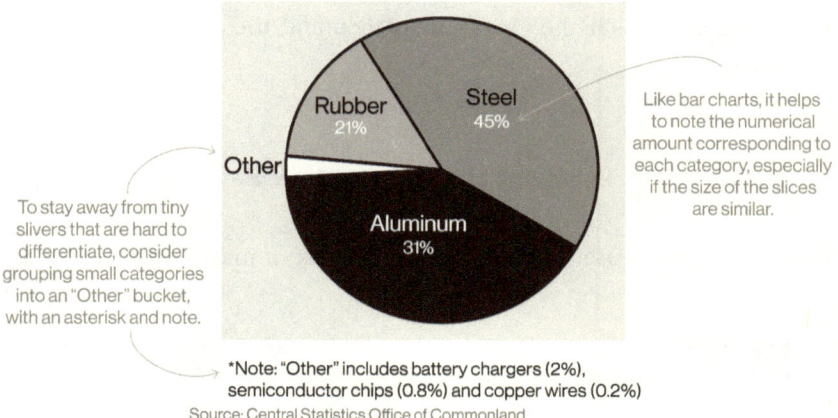

FIGURE 9.4 Pie chart

Other forms of chart and graphics include the stacked horizontal bar, the histogram, the heatmap, the pictogram, the cartogram, the dot plot, the bubble chart and the step chart.

Seven Tips for Creating Useful Charts and Graphs

- **Sketch** on a piece of paper what you want the chart or graph to convey and look like. Or ask an expert what's the most appropriate form of graphic to get across a certain idea. Decide at the outset which data are most important and need to be highlighted. Simple designs work best.
- Only add labels that help the reader or viewer **interpret** the data.
- Avoid bogging down graphs or charts with too many arrows, colors, circles or other **annotation** devices. Less is more.
- Similarly, avoid **underannotating**. The reader or viewer needs to know whether, for example, a figure is in millions or billions and in which currency. Don't assume this is obvious.
- Always include **sources**. It's imperative to say where the data came from. Remember that you may need **permission** from the source to use the data.

- Always **fact-check** and **edit** every chart in the same way that you would copy edit a story. Ask a colleague to backread the information.
- Double check that the chart's **headline** and the accompanying data are consistent.

Improving Charts: Some Examples

Enhance a graph's usefulness by adding context or making comparisons.

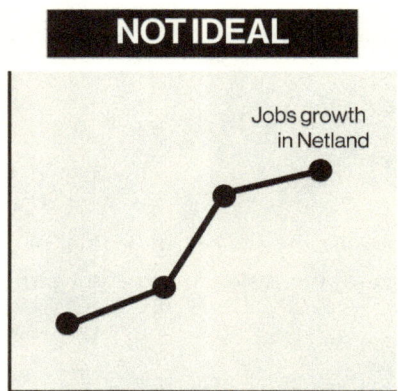 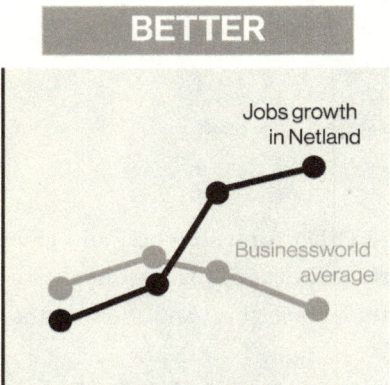

Stacked vertical charts are often better than pie charts when the size of each slice is unclear.

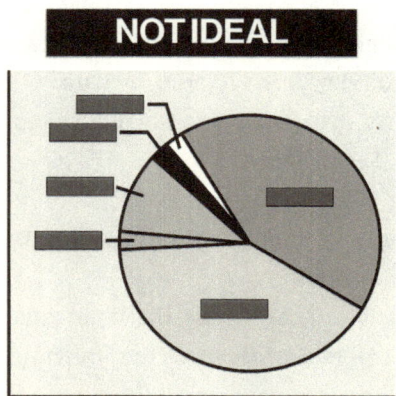 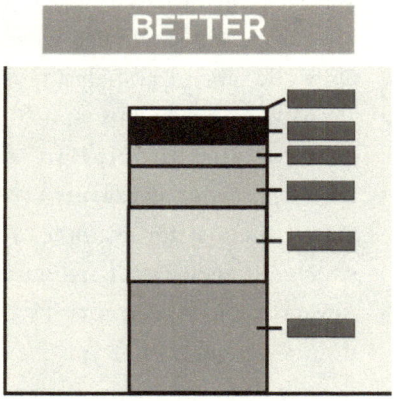

Line charts are often better than stacked vertical charts when comparing one or more variables.

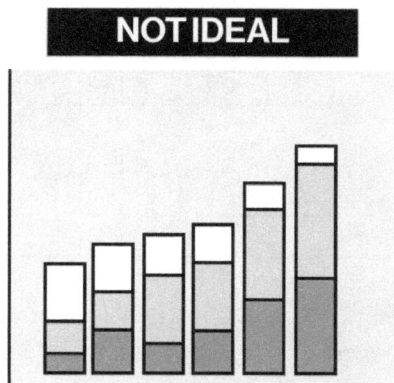
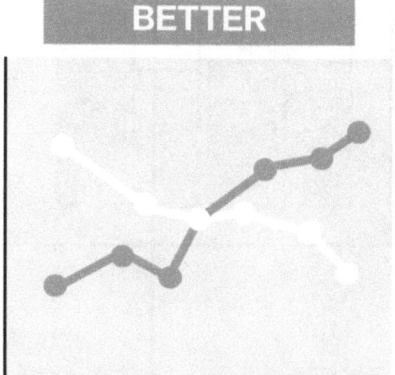

YOUR TURN 9.5 In the following examples, explain why the chart on the right is superior to the chart on the left of the page.

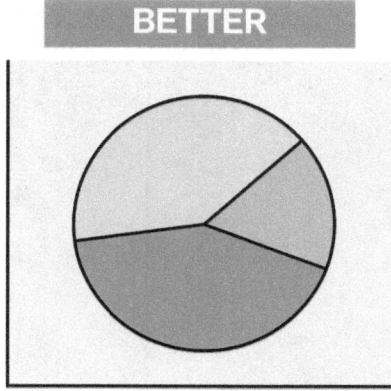

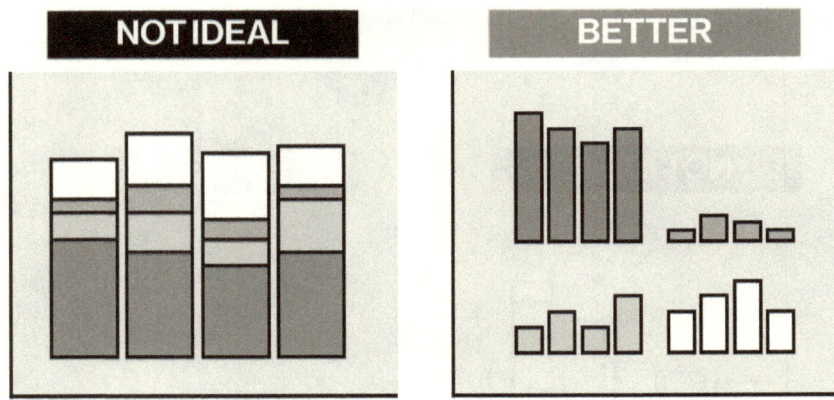

The Final Word

Data journalism is changing rapidly and comes in many forms and levels of complexity. Business journalists should embrace this fast-growing and increasingly important branch of journalism to reveal untold stories and to offer better interpretation and context.

Charts, infographics and other visual images are integral to business stories. Each image should be an independent mini-story in itself and contribute to the totality of any narrative.

Epilogue

GETTING THE JOB

The emergence of digital news technologies and data analysis tools has been a boon for business journalism. New categories of jobs that didn't exist a decade ago offer opportunities to create content and to devise and deliver new ways of reporting and telling stories.

Yet the core principles of business journalism haven't changed over the years and are unlikely to in the future. Business journalists will always need to **follow the money**, to **break news**, to **marry words with data**, to **get the story right** and to provide **objective, authoritative insight**.

What's the best way to break into this competitive field? Most reputable news organizations offer some kind of internship or apprenticeship program, and many welcome student journalists for work experience. There's no better way of learning the trade and, equally important, of making the contacts needed to secure a job.

Interns are typically recent college graduates or in their last year of study. Internships are usually for several weeks or months, during which the participants may work on various desks or beats such as covering the stock market or the local economy.

Apprentices often work at a news organization for a year or more. They're usually younger employees, without a college degree, who learn the ropes of business journalism through intensive on-the-job training.

As you embark on your career, it's important to explore what type of business journalism interests you and consider your ultimate goal. Do you want to one day be the **editor-in-chief**, running an entire newsroom of reporters and editors? Or a **senior reporter** breaking news live on air, or a **features writer** covering issues in-depth for magazines or specialist websites?

Some beginning journalists find success at niche publications such as **financial newsletters** or **trade publications**. These roles may require you to write about a specific area of business and become a subject matter expert.

The industry also offers a wide variety of roles beyond reporter and editor, so keep an open mind. For example, many newsrooms need TV, radio and podcast producers, guest bookers, social-media wizards, video editors, graphic designers and data experts, just to name a few areas.

In all of these cases, **impeccable news judgment** is vital. Journalists need the instinctive ability to know what a story is and to highlight the most compelling and surprising news amid the tsunami of content that floods newsrooms every day.

Combine that news judgment with an ability to turn complex issues into easy-to-understand content for any media platform and you will go far in this field. Our hope is that the lessons and exercises in this book will set you on a path to finding your dream job—and to breaking lots of news once you land it!

• • • •

Appendix 1

WORDS TO WATCH

American English, British English

This book was written in American English. But be aware of the differences between American English and British English. Spelling often separates the two languages.

U.S.-based news organizations use standard American-English spellings no matter where a word originates, such as **"color,"** "humor," "theater," "meager," "analyze" and "organize." Some news organizations use British-English equivalents: **"colour,"** "humour," "theatre," "meagre," "analyse" and "organise."

Some words have different meanings on opposite sides of the Atlantic. In American English, **"torrid"** means scorching or passionate: "The couple had a torrid love affair." "Inject Inc. sales set a torrid pace in Commonland, growing for 19 successive quarters." In British English, torrid means difficult: "The company had a torrid year."

In American English, **"scheme"** may imply illegal or unethical behavior. In British English, it simply means a plan, program or proposal. British companies often talk about "turnover," which in American English means "revenue" or "sales."

Overused Words and Phrases

Many words and phrases used in business journalism are redundant or require more precision. A few examples:

Boost business, boost revenue. Such phrases are often cited as reasons for a company's expansion. Be more specific or remove.

Before:

Drilling Co. plans to invest E$20 billion to *boost its business* in Energyland in the next five years as the nation opens up its economy to more foreign investors.

After:

Drilling Co. plans to invest E$20 billion in Energyland in the next five years as the nation opens its economy to more foreign investors.

Comes as, comes after. This transitional phrase is an overused crutch and can often be removed.
Before:

This move comes after the central bank last week quashed speculation that it may raise interest rates at its next meeting.

After:

The central bank last week quashed speculation that it may raise interest rates at its next meeting.

Currently, to date, now, so far. These words are often redundant.

Before:

Energyland has so far discovered more than 50 trillion cubic feet of natural gas and is currently engaging international oil companies on the terms of developing an LNG project.

After:

Energyland has discovered more than 50 trillion cubic feet of natural gas and is talking to oil companies about developing an LNG project.

Respectively. This word often takes away the momentum of a sentence, forcing the reader to reread it.
Before:

Two more financial institutions—Investing Inc. and Savings Co.—are set to report earnings this week, on Tuesday and Thursday respectively.

After:

Two more financial institutions are set to report earnings this week—Investing Inc. on Tuesday and Savings Co. on Thursday.

Non-news: No Surprise

Continue, ongoing, remain, little changed, steady, flat. These words imply there's no news because nothing significant has changed. Look for a new element and focus on that.

As expected. Say who's expecting: A company? A think tank? A government? A minister? Economists? Analysts?

Cautious. Try to avoid. People and companies are always cautious.

Vague

Abroad, foreign, overseas. These words are unclear unless the reader knows which country is being cited.

Double-digit. Could be anything from 10 to 99. Try to be more specific.

Demand. From where? From who? For what?

Early retirement, retrench, lay off. Be careful with these euphemisms. Try to say whether workers are leaving the company or institution voluntarily or not.

Green. Every company, government and institution professes to be environmentally friendly and awash with sustainability initiatives. Give specifics and provide expert voices to avoid corporate PR fluff. Write about the problem areas, proposed solutions, winners, losers and the cost.

Growth. In sales? Profit? Shipments? Economic growth?

Price target. Be specific about the time frame, which is usually 12 months.

Reform, reorganize, restructure, revitalize. These words imply an improvement, which often isn't the case. Be skeptical and give specific examples of what the company or government is actually doing.

Short term, long term. In the next month or quarter? Over the next 30 years?

Valuations. Explain what specific valuations are being cited, such as dividend yield, price/earnings ratio, price/cash flow ratio.

Take Care with the Following

Verbs

Admits, claims, concedes, explained, says, warns. Says and said are neutral, nonjudgmental verbs. Substitutes can imply bias and should be used with caution.

Believes, feels, hopes, thinks. We only know what people say and do, not what they believe, feel, hope and think. Companies don't feel or hope.

Conjunctions and Prepositions

Although, but, despite, however, since, while. Sentences beginning with conjunctions such as "although" and "while" or with prepositions such as "despite," "since" and "with" often precede a more compelling or interesting clause that deserves more attention. Flipping the sentence or breaking it in two can give the paragraph more impact.

Before:

While Snackable is still the leader in the food processing sector, Peasplus's market share has more than tripled the past two years and it's now the second-largest maker.

After:

Peasplus's market share of the food processing industry has more than tripled the past two years and it's now the second-largest maker, behind Snackable.

Relative Pronouns

Who or whom? These are different forms of the same pronoun. Who is the subject form, and whom is the object form. Who is the equivalent of he, she or they. Whom is the equivalent of him, her or them. To determine which to use, run a substitution test. Say "he" or "him" instead of "who" or "whom."

Examples:

- Is it: Whom did you speak to? or Who did you speak to? The test: Did you speak to him? Or: Did you speak to he? "Him" is correct, so use "whom."
- Is it: The president, who we thought was quiet, started shouting. Or: The president, whom we thought was quiet, started shouting. The test:

We know she is quiet. Or: We know her is quiet. "She" is correct, so use "who." The same principle applies for whoever or whomever.

Names

People want to read and hear about people—winners and losers, guilty and acquitted, victors and victims. The bigger the name, the bigger the audience. There's a truism in business journalism that says Names Make News.

But beware. Big names don't always make news. The biggest company names and the top business and political leaders in one country are often unknown elsewhere. That's when it may be preferable to describe the entity or the person rather than using the name itself. It all depends on the intended audience.

Cliches and Journalese

Banal and overused words and phrases are the bane of journalism. Use of cliches, journalese, puns and cheesy wordplay cheapen stories and suggest lazy, thoughtless writing as the italicized words below show:

Billionaire Investors in Snackable's IPO Get *Early Christmas Present*

Political Uncertainty *Muddies Waters* for Foodland's Drowning Economy

Airport Costs *Skyrocket* as Flightco Construction Plans *Take Off*

Exhausted Negotiators Hammer Out Bridge Contract at *11th Hour*

Hype

A headline should never promise more than it delivers. Understatement confers greater authority than hype. Avoid clickbait—headlines designed solely to generate more readership—and exaggerated headlines.

The original headline below forced readers to click into the story to find the news.

Before:

Prepare for a Lot More Bad News to Hit Emerging Markets This Year

After:

El Nino Threatens More Disruption, Destruction in Emerging Markets

Jargon

When a writer doesn't understand what she's writing, most readers won't, either. The following leads don't work because they contain too much jargon and too few specifics.

Before:

Sweeti Inc. Chief Executive Officer Ivan Murphy said that *continued attention to margins* in the company's *core* sugar business will yield a *competitive advantage* longer term.

After:

Sweeti Inc. Chief Executive Officer Ivan Murphy said he hoped to increase the operating margin in the company's sugar business to 14 percent this year.

Before:

The prospect of an oncoming recession has *bond bulls ratcheting up long positions* on some of Commonland's safest debt.

After:
Some regional money managers are preparing for a possible recession by buying more of Commonland's safest debt.

Commonly Used (and Abused) Style and Terms

Most errors in business journalism occur when **names** of companies and people are misspelled or misidentified and when incorrect **numbers** are published. The following are often-misunderstood style issues and business terms.

HYPHENS

Credit-default swap

> First-quarter profit (the words "first quarter" modify the word "profit")
> Health-care (adjective) but health care (noun)
> Pretax (not pre-tax)
> Private equity firm (no hyphen)
> Real estate market (no hyphen when used as a modifier)
> Small-business owner (not small business owner)
> Wi-Fi (not wifi, Wi-fi or wi-fi)

MAKER

One syllable, one word. More than one syllable, two words:

> Shipmaker, steelmaker, sausage maker, textile maker.
> Exception: automaker. Maker is preferred to manufacturer.

MONTH-ON-MONTH, QUARTER-ON-QUARTER, YEAR-ON-YEAR

These terms can easily be misunderstood.

Month-on-month (MoM or m/m) means a comparison between data from one month and the previous month (e.g., October compared with September or February with January). MoM is usually used in economic data when the numbers have been seasonally adjusted. That means they've been adjusted for the time of year, the number of weekends and the number of days in the month. Otherwise, it would be impossible to compare February (28 days or 29 days in a leap year) with January (31 days). When economic numbers are not seasonally adjusted (nsa), a MoM comparison is inappropriate.

Quarter-on-quarter (QoQ or q/q) means comparing one quarter (July/August/September, for example) with the previous quarter (April/May/June). It's frequently used to compare economic data such as gross domestic product (GDP).

However, when comparing companies' quarterly numbers, use the data from the same period a year earlier. For example, compare the first quarter this year with the first quarter last year.

Year-on-year (YoY or y/y) compares one month with the same month a year earlier. In many cases, countries report both the month-on-month and the year-on-year figures at the same time.

Examples:

Commonland Sept. CPI Rises 0.6 Percent Y/Y
Commonland Sept. CPI Rises 0.1 Percent M/M

The first headline means Commonland's consumer price index rose 0.6 percent in September compared with September a year earlier. The second means that the index rose 0.1 percent in September compared with August.

NUMBERS

Most business journalism organizations follow these conventions:

- Write "one" to "nine" as words and write numerals for 10 or more: three people, six banks, 10 companies, 14 airlines.

- Write the 1 to 9 numerals when the number precedes a currency, a unit of measurement or a ratio: 9 cents. 8-meter wall. 2-for-1 stock split.
- Round up or down to two decimal places when the number is less than 10 and precedes the word million, billion or trillion: 7.45 million. When the number is 10 or higher, round to one decimal place: 645.8 billion, 10.7 trillion.

PERCENT AND PERCENTAGE POINTS

They're not the same.

There are 100 basis points in one percentage point. In other words, 25 basis points equals a quarter of a percentage point, or 0.25 percentage point.

Central banks often increase or reduce interest rates by 0.25 percentage point, not by 0.25 percent or by 25 percent. An interest-rate increase from 2 percent to 2.5 percent is a 0.5-percentage-point increase, or 50 basis points.

ROUNDING

Round percentages of less than 10 to one decimal place: 3.4 percent, not 3.43 percent. Round up or down to a whole number for percentages of 10 or more unless more precision is warranted: 17 percent, not 17.2 percent; 29 percent, not 28.6 percent. The only exceptions are for economic data. Don't round off economic data such as GDP, inflation and Purchasing Managers Index (PMI). Report them the way they have been released.

PROFIT

Net income is the so-called bottom line in a company's income statement. Most financial news organizations look at the profitability measure that's called **net income attributable to common shareholders, adjusted.**

Companies report many kinds of profit, making it difficult to know which one to include in a story. If in doubt, ask analysts who track the company's performance. Other measures include operating profit; pre-tax profit; earnings before interest, taxes, depreciation and amortization; profit before extraordinary items; profit from continuing operations; net income on the basis of generally accepted accounting principles (GAAP); and adjusted net income.

Understanding which profitability measure to cite is critical because investors and analysts closely track a company's earnings per share, or EPS (net income divided by the number of outstanding shares); its price/earnings ratio, or P/E ratio (the price of a share divided by earnings per share); and various profitability margins.

TIME

2 P.M., not 2:00 P.M. or 2 PM.
Dec. 15, not 15th Dec., December 15 or 15th December.

TITLES

Uppercase when the title comes directly before a name; for example, MD Inc. Chairman Markus Devi. Lowercase in other circumstances; for example, Marcus Devi, chairman of MD Inc.

Appendix 2

BLOOMBERG TERMINAL FUNCTIONS FOR JOURNALISTS

There are two kinds of functions on the Bloomberg Terminal: **ticker and tail** functions, and **stand-alone** functions.

How to Find Data Using Ticker and Tail Commands

- On any Bloomberg panel, **type** what you are looking for **in simple language** in the command line. For example, *China GDP* or *crude oil* or *South Africa bonds*.
- Wait for the drop down (known as **autocomplete**) and click the appropriate **"ticker"** from the "securities" section.
- When you click on the ticker, you are **"loading"** that ticker on that panel. The gray box on the top left of the screen shows the "loaded security."
- Next to the "loaded security," another box says **"related functions."** These are the **"tail"** functions—a menu of functions related to the loaded security that can be run after loading a security. To run a tail function, click on any tail function and press ENTER (or GO on the Bloomberg keyboard).
- Two common tail functions, used across all asset classes, are **HCP** and **GP**. HCP shows historical closing prices in a table format including percentage change and volume (when applicable). GP is a representation of closing prices in the form of a chart.

- Explore **"related functions"** to go deeper into any loaded security. If you can remember a tail function, simply load the security and type the tail function and hit GO—instead of using the "related functions" tab route.

How to Find Data Using Stand-alone Functions

Data on the Bloomberg Terminal are also stored under a second kind of function that "stands alone." A stand-alone function name is just a mnemonic and doesn't involve any ticker or tail function.

All the stand-alone functions can be seen by typing **MAIN**.

In MAIN, the "Markets" section highlights functions under the various asset classes. For example, click "Sovereign" to see the stand-alone functions on government bonds.

For a snapshot of the various **asset classes**, here are some key stand-alone functions:

WEI shows real-time price and volume data for the world's primary equity indexes, and the relative value, for example, of price-to-earnings ratios and dividend yield.

WB lists benchmark bonds of countries, showing their prices, yields, spreads and curves.

WCRS ranks and compares current and historical currency rates on a bar chart, making it easy to identify, analyze and understand foreign exchange market trends, interest rates, volatility and purchasing power.

GLCO shows real-time benchmark prices of all commodities.

GEW, or global economy watch, monitors and displays key economic data for countries around the world.

Search Functions

Some stand-alone functions can be used to create **powerful searches of data**. For example, business journalists, investors and other Bloomberg Terminal users look at these tools to find which company has the biggest stockpile of cash or which company has the most bonds maturing this year or to find the biggest merger and acquisition (M&A) deal announced this year.

EQS can be used to **analyze equities (companies)**. The idea is to narrow the universe of equities to a group that you'd like to analyze—such as companies in a certain country or on a specific stock index. Then, apply a criteria, like P/E or cash balance.

IPO aggregates data on **initial public offerings** worldwide. Filter by region, country, industry or other criteria. Click into any IPO for details such as the number of shares offered, the price, timeline, structure and advisers.

MA aggregates data on **mergers and acquisitions** worldwide. Filter by region, country, industry or other criteria. Rank M&A by criteria such as the announced value and ratio of the transaction value to earnings. Click into any individual M&A for details about the target and the acquirer, the transaction value, key dates, structure and advisers.

ECST shows world **economic statistics**.

FSRC, or the **fund search** function, makes it possible to identify the smartest fund managers in various asset classes who can offer intelligent analysis and commentary for stories.

SRCH can be used to **analyze bond sales**. For example, it can show which country or company has the most bonds maturing this year, or has issued the most bonds in the past year, the average yields, the maturity profile and so on.

LEAG ranks banks that have managed the **biggest bond sales** or **IPO**s in the current year. Make historical comparisons to see data such as which bank is the biggest manager of bond sales in a certain country this year and how that compares with previous years.

Other Useful Functions

BI, or **Bloomberg Intelligence**, is a comprehensive source for news, data and analysis on companies, industries and economies by Bloomberg analysts.

CRPR shows the **credit rating profile of a company**: how each of the major rating companies assesses the borrower's willingness and ability to repay its debt.

CSDR lists the **credit rating of countries**, including historical changes.

DVD shows a company's **dividend payment history**.

ECO shows economic statistics in every country. See estimates for announcements on economic output, inflation, unemployment and other data released monthly, quarterly and annually.

ERN collects the key **earnings and estimates** data, highlighting how a company has fared historically in relation to the expectations of the investing community.

EQRV shows how a company is **valued relative to its peers**, given its historical performance on selected multiples as compared to the group.

ETF shows **exchange-traded funds**, broken down by specific asset classes, regions, indexes, industries and fund objectives.

FA allows **financial analysis** of any listed company, including income statements, balance sheets and cash-flow statements.

FIRV is the **fixed-income relative value** page. Load a specific bond and compare the yield and price with peers. Compare the spread, or difference, between this bond's yield and the benchmark of the country.

HLDS shows the **key stock holdings** of companies, funds and other investors for a perspective on their investment and business strategies.

MADL shows a company's **M&A profile**, including assets sold and acquired, the value and deal status.

RATD shows **rating scales and definitions**: the assessments by ratings companies of the ability of borrowers to repay their debt. The ratings typically fall into two broad categories: investment grade, meaning they're unlikely to default, and non-investment grade for borrowers posing a higher risk of nonpayment.

News and Analysis on the Bloomberg Terminal

BTDY shows the **most important stories** in the world in real time, as well as top podcasts, research, opinion, video, features and most-read stories.

TOP is Bloomberg's curated front page.

N means news about a certain topic. For specific news, type N followed by key words. For example: N TESLA EARNINGS shows news about Tesla's earnings. N US CHINA TRADE BLOOMBERG shows trade stories about the United States and China published by Bloomberg.

DAYB, or Daybreak, is a real-time electronic newspaper, curated regionally.

FIRS offers customized news focused on specific asset classes for Bloomberg Terminal customers.

MEDI is the main multimedia function. Click to see Bloomberg interactive TV, radio, podcasts and webinars.

OPIN shows Bloomberg Opinion editorials and columns.

NH BBG shows all content from Bloomberg Editorial and Research in one place: **NH BI** for Bloomberg Intelligence; **NH NEF** for Bloomberg New Energy Finance; **NH** for all sources.

Appendix 3

TEACHING GUIDE FOR ONE-DAY, ONE-WEEK AND 10-WEEK TRAINING COURSES

One Day

Consider hosting four sessions of 75 minutes each, with the goal of conveying what business journalism is and how it's practiced.

- Session 1: What's business journalism? Why does it matter?
- Session 2: How to break business news on topics from markets and companies to the economy.
- Session 3: What's news? An introduction to business writing, focusing on the headline and the first four paragraphs of a story.
- Session 4: The various ways of telling a business story—from headlines and written narratives to TV, radio, podcasts and other multimedia formats.

One Week

A one-week class offers scope to discuss ethics and standards in journalism, to introduce the Bloomberg Terminal and to share basic ideas on how to generate content in various formats to cover financial markets, companies and the economy. The proposal below assumes four classes a day of 75 minutes each.

- Day 1: What's business journalism and why does it matter? An introduction to the Bloomberg Terminal. Ethics and standards.
- Day 2: The basics of covering companies, stocks, bonds, commodities and the economy.
- Day 3: The newsroom. From headlines to deadlines. Explain and explore various ways of telling a story (headlines, charts, podcasts, TV, radio, photos, blogs and so on). The fundamentals of writing business journalism. Timed drills.
- Day 4: Multimedia. Skills for TV and radio. Writing for the web and social media. Timed drills.
- Day 5: How to interview like a professional. How to build sources and break news. The art of getting a great job: how to present yourself as a job candidate. Mock job interview.

10 Weeks or More

Use this book to cover the wide range of topics in business journalism. The proposal below assumes one or two classes a week. Begin each session by critiquing the main stories in business newspapers, magazines and websites. **Incorporate writing drills into every class.**

- **Week 1:** What's business journalism and why does it matter? What's news and news judgment? An introduction to writing business stories. How to capture the surprise in the headline and weave the first four paragraphs of a story. Explore the various formats of telling a business story—from flash headlines and writing long-form narratives to multimedia. Ethics and standards in business journalism.
- **Week 2:** Stock market coverage. How a stock is created to secondary-market trading. Teach essential concepts such as valuations and basic technical analysis.

- **Week 3:** Company coverage 1. How to cover corporate actions such as earnings, mergers and acquisitions, buybacks, stock splits and dividends.
- **Week 4:** Company coverage 2. Focus on how to read financial statements. Discuss the differences between writing spot stories and enterprise/feature stories about companies. How to build sources. The art of interviewing.
- **Week 5:** Covering the economy. Covering economic indicators and proxy indicators. How to write about monetary and fiscal policy. How to report on currencies. How to tell stories using charts.
- **Week 6:** Bond market coverage. How to report on government and corporate bonds, yields and spreads. The importance of credit ratings. Discuss credit-default swaps.
- **Week 7:** Commodities coverage. How to report on hard and soft commodities and the companies that extract the minerals or grow the crops.
- **Week 8:** Best practices for online journalism. The basic tenets of digital/multimedia journalism. Understanding audiences and how to target them to build your site and brand. How to present a story on social-media platforms.
- **Week 9:** Best practices in television and radio. How to write a TV and radio script. How to talk with authority. Presentation skills. Mock interviews and panel discussions.
- **Week 10:** Connecting the dots. A course wrap. A review of the various asset classes and how to report on them. A review of ways to write and produce content for different platforms.

Answer Key for "Your Turn" Exercises

Most answers to Your Turn questions could be written several ways. Apart from mathematical calculations, there are no "right" or "wrong" answers. The answers here are simply suggestions.

Chapter 1

Answer 1.1

For the Energyland preschool story, one could explore the following angles:

a. Find out how many people could lose their jobs because of this.
b. Find out whether the government will reallocate the funds to another program.
c. Consider whether the move will result in a lower budget deficit. That may result in fewer government bond sales, pushing bond prices higher and yields lower.

For increasing rents:

a. Find out whether a 30 percent increase is higher or lower than in similar apartment buildings in Netland. If higher, what's the justification?

b. Have any tenants decided to move in light of the higher rents? If so, where to? Interview them.
c. On average, what percentage of peoples' salaries are being spent on rent? Do the increases mean residents need to cut back on food or other things? Ask local government for data. Interview local residents.

For avocado toast:

a. Find out what impact this craze has had on demand for avocados and pineapple marmalade.
b. Where do these products come from and what impact, if any, has the craze had on the suppliers/growers/producers? Interview them.
c. Interview restaurants serving this meal about the business impact. More customers? More profit? Difficulties in getting supplies?

For women's wages:

a. Find out whether this holds true for other factories in Supplyland.
b. Look for data to figure out whether 90 cents is higher than five or 10 years ago? Is the gap narrowing, widening or static?
c. Interview women's groups, labor unions and other organizations about the disparity. Get comments from the factory owner.

For Businessworld Olympics:

a. Interview government officials about the likely financial impact of holding the Olympics.
b. Examine statistics from previous Olympics to find out the expected cost and financial benefits from holding the games.
c. Find out the corporate sponsorships for the games, how much each sponsor will be paying, and which sports and athletes will benefit most financially from being involved.

ANSWER KEY FOR "YOUR TURN" EXERCISES • 219

Answer 1.2

Example of turning a local story into one with global appeal:

My hometown will host the world athletic championship in six months. To prepare, the local government has been investing in roads, the subway and a new airport over the past 10 years.

Labor in my hometown/country is cheap. With the infrastructure on a level with the best anywhere, some of the world's biggest companies plan to invest in factories and open offices in my hometown.

I will interview local and national government officials (in charge of giving licenses to overseas companies); companies that are most likely to invest; real estate brokers; and fund managers who invest in stocks and bonds in my country.

Answer 1.3

No journalist should write such a letter. Avoid putting sensitive exchanges with your sources in writing. Whenever possible, meet your sources in person to confirm a story or gather news.

Any form of electronic message can be shared or hacked—and could expose your sources. In the event of litigation, you may be asked to submit all your correspondence. Be mindful of what you say on telephone calls, which can be recorded.

The long list of problems in the letter include: revealing that the source has previously given information to the reporter; defamation of the chief financial officer; offering the source something (a meal and champagne) in exchange for the information; revealing information that the reporter has received off-the-record; and revealing when the story will be published.

Chapter 2

Answer 2.1

Sip Aims to Raise as Much as F$20 Million From IPO for Factory

Sip Corp. plans to raise as much as F$20 million from an initial public offering to help build a second factory in Foodland.

The energy-drinks maker will sell 500,000 shares at a price band of F$30 to F$40, according to an advertisement in the *Foodland Times* newspaper.

After the IPO, the founders' 100 percent stake in Sip will drop to 80 percent. Foodland Bank is the lead manager of the IPO.

Answer 2.2

It's been an excellent start for Sip on the Foodland Stock Exchange today, with its stock jumping 16 percent within minutes of its trading debut. This high demand for Sip's shares indicates investor optimism for the energy-drink maker, which plans to build a second factory in Foodland. Some investors said that Sip's initial trading price was cheap relative to its earnings potential. Sip sold its shares for F$35 apiece in its IPO. Its shares closed tonight at F$39.55.

Answer 2.3

a. 32 × 1,000,000 = F$32 million
b. 25.70 × 1,200,000 = F$30.84 million
c. Snackable's market capitalization has risen F$104 million this year:

30 × 5,200,000 = F$156 million
10 × 5,200,000 = F$52 million
F$156 million − F$52 million = F$104 million

Answer 2.4

Fex Climbs to Record, Led by Peasplus, on Earnings Optimism in Foodland

Foodland's Fex Index climbed to a record after Peasplus Corp. posted better-than-expected profit, fueling earnings optimism among investors.

Peasplus's earnings are "a harbinger of good times for corporate Foodland," said Michelle Chua, managing director and market strategist at Toe Stock Broking Co. in Teaville. She said she plans to raise her earnings estimates for Foodland's other companies "which at the moment seem very conservative." Peasplus is a bellwether stock in Foodland because it's usually the first major company to report its quarterly profits.

The Fex Index jumped 3.8 percent to close at an all-time high of 1,516.35. Peasplus, which said the sales outlook for next year was "very strong," jumped 4.6 percent to a record F$26.

Peasplus's upbeat results prompted brokerage houses such as Cheese Analysis Inc. and Butter Analytics Co. to consider raising their net income predictions for other companies. Foodland, whose economy depends on agriculture, is benefiting from a bumper harvest this year.

Chapter 3

Answer 3.1

The extra yield investors demanded to hold Inject's 2.3 percent bond maturing in November 2032, compared with Netland's government debt of similar maturity, narrowed five basis points in the past 10 days to 115.5 basis points.

Answer 3.2

Wear to Split Stock 2-for-1 to Attract More Investors

Wear Inc., the biggest clothing company in Supplyland, will split its stock 2-for-1 to make it easier for investors to buy the stock.

The shares are being split to "create additional liquidity and attract a broad range of investors," Wear said in a statement. The split is effective Aug. 23.

There will be no change in the company's dividend forecast.

Answer 3.3

a. Web is offering (N$60 × 0.7 = N$42) + 10 = N$52 a share
b. Web's total offer = N$52 × 1.123 billion = N$58.39 billion
c. Web's premium: N$52/N$50 = 1.04

1.04 − 1 × 100 = 4 percent premium

Answer 3.4

Fizz Sales Rise Most in 10 Years on New Low-Sugar Drinks; Shares Soar

Fizz Co. sales jumped the most in 10 years last quarter as an advertising campaign for new low-sugar drinks proved a hit with teenagers and young adults. The stock rose 10 percent.

Fizz invested F$100 million in the past two years to develop beverages such as Van Fizz and Cool Fizz after revenue from its traditional sugary soft drinks stagnated, the company said in a statement.

"We waited a long time for Fizz's new products to finally bear fruit," said Park Won Wei, a money manager with Get Rich Asset Management Co. in Fund City, Bankland. "Sales will only get better." The fund holds 6 million Fizz shares.

For investors, the future prospects of the new drinks outweighed a drop in quarterly profit. In the fourth quarter, sales rose 8.1 percent to F$5.18 billion, more than double its 4 percent forecast. Net income fell 3 percent to F$622 million, the first decline in 18 months, on higher advertising and development costs.

Answer 3.5

Here is how one can report the clothing company story:

- Seek access and visit the clothing company's factory to ascertain whether the non-governmental organization's (NGO's) accusations are correct.
- Speak with the management, factory workers and trade union leaders and ask about the NGO's claims.
- Cultivate sources in the company who can offer more information.
- Check with relevant government authorities/regulators.
- Speak with top legal firms involved with labor laws.
- Check with fund managers who've bought and sold the company's shares.
- Speak with the top analysts covering the company.
- Make inquiries to the company's bankers and auditors.
- Check with the company's competitors to see if they have any information about the issue.

Chapter 4

Answer 4.1

Here is an example:
The economy may slow in the coming quarters. My hypothesis is based on the following facts:

- Two malls shut their operations in the capital city.
- The latest inflation reading shows prices climbed for an 11th month.

- The central bank yesterday raised interest rates for the third time in the past year and said its "battle with inflation" isn't over.
- Three families I interviewed recently said that they've cut nonessential spending such as eating in restaurants.
- The country's biggest automaker recently announced job cuts.

Answer 4.2

Bankland's Growth Falters Just as Vipervirus Forces Factory Closures

Bankland's economy expanded at its weakest pace in four years and may deteriorate further as the spiraling vipervirus crisis forced hundreds of companies to close their factories.

The vipervirus, which spreads from human contact, has claimed more than 1,000 lives since its outbreak in January. Most businesses in the country's central region, which accounts for half of Bankland's factories, have shut temporarily. Gross domestic product rose 1.8 percent in the fourth quarter compared with the previous three months.

Economic expansion could slow to 0.5 percent this quarter, said Brian Fernandez, the nation's top equity fund manager. Minutes after the data were released, Bankland's central bank said it will maintain an "accommodative" stance, meaning that it will keep interest rates low. The bank also called for greater coordination between monetary and fiscal policies to support growth, saying the "central bank cannot be the only game in town."

"There is an urgent need for a concerted stimulus package," said Fernandez, who manages B$100 million of stocks at Growth Asset Management Co. in Fund City. "Otherwise, it will be hard to arrest this slide in growth." He expects the central bank to cut its key rate and the cash reserve ratio by 50 basis points in its March 5 policy statement.

Bankland's central bank has lowered its benchmark policy rate by a percentage point in the past six months.

Government spending rose 0.48 percent last quarter, the slowest pace in three years. That's because a weakening economy has cut tax revenue, leaving the government with little money to spend on infrastructure.

Answer 4.3

Exercise 1

Smart Speakers, Dog Treats Debut in Foodland Inflation Shopping Basket
Smart speakers, dog treats, flavored tea and electric toothbrushes are among items that Foodland's statistics office has included in a revamped consumer price index to reflect changes in goods and services bought by people.

The new items "represent specific markets where consumer spending is significant or growing," according to a report from the nation's National Statistics Office.

Other headline possibilities:

Envelopes Ejected From Foodland Inflation Shopping Basket as Snailmail Slumps
Higher Tech Spending Prompts Tweaks in Foodland Inflation Shopping Basket

Exercise 2

Television ideas:
Show how the products that have been included in the new CPI basket, such as peanut butter, electric toothbrushes and smart speakers, are stacked in shops.

Show people baking, and note that the popularity of TV cooking shows has spurred demand for bakeware.

Interview shopkeepers about changing consumption patterns. Ask shoppers to compare their shopping list today from a decade ago, and describe the changes.

Prepare an infographic to show how sales of these newly added products have been rising.

Social media idea:

Do you spoil your dog? It might be affecting the way economists measure inflation.

Exercise 3

A magazine story tracing the rise and fall of envelopes. Research the history of envelopes. Talk with executives at companies that make envelopes, mail carriers and stationery retailers.

Answer 4.4

On climate change proposals, for example, you could approach the story in a couple of ways:

a. Outline the government's climate goals and explain why any changes are significant.
b. Focus on whether the subsidies are alluring enough for consumers to embrace solar panels and home insulation.

Speak with relevant officials in the government, climate experts and consumers.

Some key questions for government officials:

How much of a subsidy will the government offer? How much higher are the subsidies from previous allocations? How will these measures enable the government to meet its climate goals? How much do you expect emissions to be cut and in what time frame?

For climate experts:

How would you view the government policy? A step in the right direction or an inadequate approach? Is there any evidence in Businessworld where such a step has succeeded in combating climate change?

For consumers:

Would you take advantage of the government subsidy and buy solar panels or home insulation? Why?

Answer 4.5

Some headline ideas:

Largest Commonland Airline Predicts First Loss if 'No Fly' Wins

'Finally, I'll Be Able to Sleep': Mother's Joy at 'No Fly' Proposal

Airline CEO Lambasts Commonland for Night Flight Restrictions

Union Sees 4,000 Airport Job Losses if Night Flight Hours Are Cut

Unions, Airlines Battle Anti-Noise Warriors Over 'No Fly' Proposal

Chapter 5

Answer 5.1

Wheat Rises to Six-Month High as Heavy Snow Hampers Exports

Wheat futures in Energyland climbed to the highest level in six months after heavy snow curtailed production of the winter crop and prevented some exports.

Contracts for April delivery rose 0.4 percent to E$5.60 a bushel. Traders predicted extreme weather would lead to waning stockpiles this year. Energyland's Department of Agriculture will release its monthly supply and demand estimates later today.

Answer 5.2

The answers could include mention of graphs, charts, tables, photos and other multimedia images related to Bankland's infrastructure spending, strikes and Build's share-price movement.

Answer 5.3

Commonland Oil Exports Face Further Delay on Lack of Funds for Pipelines

Or

Commonland Unlikely to Export Oil for at Least Four Years, Prime Minister Says
Commonland's plans to export crude oil will probably be delayed again because of the cost and complexity involved in building pipelines, Prime Minister Greg Ravi said today.

A decade after discovering oil, Commonland still needs at least four more years before it can begin exporting the commodity, Ravi said in an interview. The "timetable may need to be adjusted," he said.

Pureoil Co. fell 1.9 percent and Commonland Refinery Corp. dropped 2.1 percent after the interview. The Commonland dollar weakened 0.8 percent per Energyland dollar.

Answer 5.4

Gold May Keep Falling as Energyland Jobs Data Seen Spurring Risk
A gold selloff deepened before data that may show Energyland's unemployment rate fell for a sixth month, a trend that's prompting a rush out of haven assets.

The precious metal slid 1.4 percent to E$1,949 per ounce, bringing the drop this year to 7.6 percent. Jobs data for January will probably show the unemployment rate in Businessworld's richest economy declined for a sixth month to 3.2 percent, according to the median forecast of 27 economists. The data will be released at 8:30 a.m. tomorrow.

"An upbeat jobs number will trigger a flight from gold," said Joshua Glitton, chief analyst at Glitton Smith Associates, who predicts the commodity could decline as low as E$1,800 an ounce this month. "Healthy jobs numbers augur well for the global economy and mean investors will be more adventurous."

Chapter 6

Answer 6.1

Sip Forecasting Highest Operating Margin in Four Years: BLTV

Sip Corp. predicts that its operating profit margin will rise to a four-year high in the third quarter as the Foodland soft-drinks company bounces back from what it called a "very tough" year.

The operating margin will increase to 18 percent next quarter from about 15 percent a year ago, Chief Financial Officer Lisa Ogawa said in an interview with BLTV today. To cut costs, Sip has slashed advertising, trimmed its management team and closed two offices, Ogawa said. Revenue is set to grow 4 percent next quarter, she added.

Sip is in talks with bankers and money managers in Bankland to help raise F$400 million through a bond sale, Chief Executive Officer Jameel Smith said. The money will be used to make the company's factories more fully automated, he said.

Answer 6.2

The efficiency ratio was 40 percent.

The new ratio rose to 46 percent. A higher ratio was bad for the bank, suggesting that costs may be getting out of control.

Answer 6.3

This answer depends on the country/market that you track.

Answer 6.4

Sip Corp. Chief Financial Officer Lisa Ogawa plans to buy F$1 million worth of Arabica coffee beans in December.

The December contract is currently trading at F$1.18 per pound. But Ogawa expects the disease ravaging coffee crops to severely hurt supplies this year. As a result, she estimates prices will rise to as much as F$1.45 by December.

To reduce Sip's import costs, Ogawa thinks it would be a good strategy to buy the current December contract and lock in the purchase at F$1.18.

Answer 6.5

This answer depends on the country/market that you track.

Chapter 7

Answer 7.1

Q1. What indication did the governor give about interest rates?
Q2. Why are you doing this?
Q3. How did it make you feel to prove your doubters wrong?
Q4. Why do you care so much about this issue?

Answer 7.2

Don't rush to report the news.
  Consult immediately with colleagues and more senior editors.
  Seek confirmation from the government and other sources.
  Consider the following: Is this the way the government would normally announce such an event? Has Ravi been in poor health?
  Look for red flags in the Squeak, such as missing or misspelled words, poor grammar or false information.

Check for any market reaction in Commonland and elsewhere.

If you're sure the news is true, send flash headlines and a two-paragraph story immediately. Check whether your news organization has prewritten an obituary for use after Ravi's death

If the news is false, write a story about how the Squeak appeared and the possible implications.

Answer 7.3

For the Netland company story:

Publish the key numbers in a table or in a bullet-point format. Include analysts' estimates when relevant. In this breaking-news situation, investors may not have time to read a long-form story. A table or bullet-point format would offer a snapshot of the key numbers.

Power outage story:

Add a map highlighting the residential areas and locations of businesses. Consider a table showing other similar outages or a list of major businesses affected by the power cut.

Foodland central bank story:

Consider charts or other graphics that highlight the "conditions" that the central bank head is talking about. The central bank may be hinting at slowing inflation or falling prices in specific constituents of the country's consumer price index.

Answer 7.4

Here are possible versions of the story:

Print

Wine Industry Threatened as Fires, Drought Ravage Foodland Region

Or

Wildfires Tear Through Foodland's Wine Country; 20,000 Evacuated

Wildfires tore through Foodland's renowned wine-producing region Monday, prompting more than 20,000 people to flee their homes and offices.

At least 200 buildings have burned down since Thursday, including the award-winning Grapeland Valley Winery. It's likely that more will be ruined because only about 10 percent of the fires have been contained, according to local fire officials.

{Insert photo of burning winery}

The fires are a consequence of too much construction near forested areas, infestations of bark beetles and other pests, water shortages and climate change, according to scientists and regional experts.

About 90 percent of land in the wine-growing region is abnormally dry and almost half of it is at some stage of drought, according to the Foodland Drought Monitor, a government agency. A year ago, 11 percent of the area was in drought, the monitor said.

The Foodland Insurance Bureau said insurance losses may top F$1 billion. This would include lost wine sales, destroyed homes and the impact on tourism. About 100,000 people work in the local wine business.

{Insert chart of estimated insurance losses and/or breakdown of visitors, wine sales}

Foodland's wine region attracted more than 10 million visitors and sold F$2 billion of wine last year, according to the Foodland Wine Institute, a consortium of vineyard owners.

TV Script

{Video of blaze destroying Grapeland Valley Winery}

Foodland's award-winning Grapeland Valley Winery burned down today as three wildfires tore through the nation's wine region.

The winery is one of more than 200 buildings destroyed by the fires, which prompted at least 20,000 people to evacuate their homes and offices.

{Reporter on camera, standing in front of a burning home, and people loading trucks with household possessions in the background}

Tens of thousands of jobs are at risk from the fires, the Chamber of Commerce here says. That's because the local wine business is one of the key drivers of the region's economy, employing 100,000 people, the chamber says.

{Video of blaze approaching dry land that is not on fire}

With no rain forecast for the immediate future, the Foodland Insurance Bureau estimates insurance losses will top 1 billion dollars.

Radio

More than 20,000 people have been evacuated from Foodland's famous wine country today as wildfires rage through the region's forests.

{Sound of fires/sound of fire engines}

At least 200 structures, including the award-winning Grapeland Valley Winery, have been destroyed.

With no rain forecast and almost half of the land in the area at some stage of drought, the Foodland Insurance Bureau estimates losses could top 1 billion dollars.

Social-Media Post

Wine industry faces $1 billion in job and other losses as wildfires ravage Foodland vineyards. Read more here.

Chapter 8

Answer 8.1

Snackable Inc. Chief Executive Officer Amelia Martin resigned today to become head of a charitable organization after overseeing seven consecutive years of sales growth.

Commonland's central bank is searching for new ways to protect the currency from further declines following the government's decision to raise tariffs.

Answer 8.2

Build Co. will renovate 10,000 state-owned homes after it agreed on a C$400 million contract with Commonland's government.

Answer 8.3

Robo Corp. is returning to Netland's bond market **_for the first time in three years_** with its **_biggest-ever offering_**.

Or

Robo Corp. is poised to issue its **_largest-ever bond_** in Netland, an N$800 million sale to help fund at least 150 new warehouses.

Answer 8.4

Choose your answers on the basis of the writing guidelines in this chapter.

Answer 8.5

Bankland Inflation May Accelerate to 6.7 Percent by December, Growth Asset Says

Sweeti to Buy Sip Sugar-Refining Business Even as Consumption Dwindles

Or

Sip to Sell Sugar-Refining Business to Sweeti as Consumer Demand Dwindles
Energyland to Double Spending on Roads, Bridges, Power in Remote Areas

Answer 8.6

Linen Shares Fall 11 Percent as "Fluffy" Cushion Fad Fades
Linen Co. shares fell the most in two years after Supplyland's largest textile maker said sales of its top-selling "Fluffy" cushions slid 20 percent from a year earlier.

Or

Linen's 'Fluffy' Sales Decline 20 Percent From Record as Cushion Fad Fades
Linen Co. sold 20 percent fewer "Fluffy" cushions last year than a year earlier in a sign that a fad for branded furnishings has faded. The shares fell 11 percent, the most in two years.

Answer 8.7

Eatmore's delay threatens Chief Executive Officer Kenji Hargreaves's plans to arrest falling profits by expanding in Energyland, where larger rival Mysteak Inc. is already adding new restaurants.

The decision leaves Eatmore dependent on the waning Netland market just as rivals Mysteak Inc. and Steak N Chips Co. are set to expand in Energyland.

Answer 8.8

Peasplus Chief Executive Officer Angela Singh said she expected the company will be making a "hefty profit" from its palm oil operations within three years, when it should be producing 50,000 tons a year.

None of the quotes are suitable. The first is self-serving and pure public relations. The second is too long and doesn't get to the point. The third is simply a statement of fact. If you really need to use such quotes, paraphrase.

Snackable is meeting prospective partners this week and hopes to conclude a deal by the end of the month, Nicky Chen, a company spokesman, said.

Chapter 9

Answer 9.1

Bankland home prices fell for a seventh month in October, declining 0.9 percent to an average of B$304,770, Houseprice Inc. said in a report Tuesday.

Inject Inc. profit rose 50 percent last year after the pharmaceuticals company introduced its first lung-cancer drug.

Answer 9.2

Auld Inc. shares fell 4.7 percent following the unexpected resignation of Chief Financial Officer Jamie Johnson.

Supplyland's trade deficit widened to a record S$214 billion in August after a surge in oil imports and a fall in exports of electronic products.

Cocoa prices rose to a more than two-year high after the Foodland government confirmed reports that an unknown disease is blighting the crop.

Answer 9.3

Power plant:

> 200 megawatts × 1 million watts/megawatt divided by 5,000 watts/home = 40,000 homes

Wear's factory:

> 200 meters × 120 meters = 24,000 square meters of factory
> 105 meters × 68 meters = 7,140 square meters of soccer pitch
> 24,000 divided by 7,140 = 3.36 soccer pitches

Sip energy drinks:

> 10 million cases × 12 bottles/case × 0.5 liters/bottle = 60 million liters of beer
> 50 meters × 25 meters × 2 meters = 2,500 cubic meters

> 2,500 cubic meters × 1,000 liters/cubic meter = 2.5 million liters in pool
> 60 million divided by 2.5 million = 24 swimming pools

Imps phones:

> 231.2 million + 211.9 million = 443.1 million phones
> 140 millimeters = 0.00014 kilometers
> 443.1 million phones × 0.00014 kilometers/phone = 62,034 kilometers
> 62,034/40,000 = 1.55 the Earth's circumference

Answer 9.4

The mean estimate was C$149 million.
The median was S$142 billion.

Answer 9.5

a. The pie chart allows readers or viewers to understand immediately how the parts make up the whole.
b. By showing four vertical bar charts, it's easier to understand the relationship of one data set to another.

Index

accounts payable, 62
accounts receivable, 62
accuracy, 13, 132, 148, 164
acquisitions, 47–48
acronyms, 162
active verbs, 154–55
active voice, 155–56
AI. *See* artificial intelligence
alliteration, 163
anchor investors, 22
anecdotes, 177
anonymous sources, 136–38
AOV. *See* average order value
apprentices, 193-94
ARPU. *See* average revenue per unit/user
artificial intelligence (AI), xi
assets: asset-backed security, 129; bonds as, 86; haven assets, 110; intangible assets, 62; net asset value, 127; net fixed assets, 61–62
attribution: in leads, 168; for reporting business stories, 144
auctions, of government bonds, 87–88, *88*
audience: headlines geared to, 159–61, 164; target, for podcasts, 145
authoritative voices, 143
automation, 3
average order value (AOV), 60
average revenue per unit/user (ARPU), 60

balance sheet, 53, 61–62
Bankland (fictional country): Build Co. example, in, 105–6, 156, 182, 234; country profile, 7; economic growth in, 165; Fund City example, in, 59, 78, 222, 224; GDP in, 75; Get Rich Asset Management Co. example, in, 59; Growth Asset Management Co. example, in, 75, 224; house prices in, 236; InsureCo Inc. example, in, 119, 120, 131; latest craze in, 9; OneBank Co. example, in, 115, 116, 118, 122; president in, 14; Savings Co. example, in, 78, 197; spending in, 228; transportation in, 159; vipervirus in, 224
bankruptcy, 130
banks, *115*; business journalists reporting on, 117–18; commercial banks, 116; earnings, 117; future strategy, 117; internet banks, 121; investment banks, 115–17; performance, 117. *See also* central banks
bar charts, 186–87, *187*
benchmarks: benchmark bond, 41–42; benchmark contract, 124; benchmark index, 24; benchmark interest rates, 71, 72, 74; benchmark price, 101
best practices, in story writing: accurate writing, 13; avoiding conflict of interest, 13; correct errors, 13; fairness, 14; no law breaking, 13; privacy and defamation, 14–15; serve public interest, 15; show, don't tell, 15
bid, 23–24
big-picture idea, 152

big-picture paragraph: for business story, 172–74; examples, 173–74; image, impact, importance conveyed in, 173; language prompts in, 173; provides relative value, 172; secondary big-picture paragraph, 176; tells what's at stake, 172
blockchain technology, 121
Bloomberg Terminal: business news functions, 209–10; news analysis on, 210–11; search functions, 208–9; stand-alone functions for data search, 208; ticker and tail commands, 207–8
bonds: benchmark bond, 41–42; bond prices, 41, 42; bond seesaw, *39*; companies selling, 35–41, 113; corporate bond ratings, 38; deep bond market in Supplyland (fictional country), 36; defined, 36; face value of, 36–38; fixed coupon rate, 38; high-yield bonds, 41; journalists tracking, 40–41; junk bonds, 40–41; making money from, 40; managing, 36; municipal bonds, 130; performance of, 41, 42, *42*; private placement of, 36; public issue of, 36–37; as safe asset, 86; sovereign bond, 38; underwriting, 36; writing about corporate bonds, 41–45; yield, spread and, 43–45; yield and, 38–39, *39*, 41. *See also* government bonds
book-building process, 22
bookrunner, 20, *20*
borrowing: by companies, 129; investments and, 129–31; long-term borrowings, 62
the bottom line, 53
brevity, 148
bubble chart, 189
budgets: budget deficit, 84; budget surplus, 84; in countries, 83–84
bullet points, 177
business confidence, 76, 95
business journalism: broad definition of, x; current broad approach in, xi; diversity in, xii; early forms of, x–xi; expertise development by, 112; 5Ws and H for, x; relevance of, ix; teaching guide, 213–15. *See also specific topics*
business journalists: apprentices, 193–94; Bloomberg Terminal functions for, 207–11; bonds tracked by, 40–41; commodities reporting by, 100–102; editor-in-chief, 194; explanatory journalists, x, 177; features writer, 194; follow the money, 1, 23, 96, 193; forward-looking comments of, 57; on hedge funds, 120, 132; interns, 193; meaning and, x; mission and role of, x; prepare for routine, 65; proxy indicators watched by, 98; qualities, for breaking stories, 34; reporting on banks, 117–18; reporting on legislation, 96; senior reporter, 194; sense for anticipating news, 54–55; source building by, 65; so what and, x; as storytellers, 167; supply and demand reporting, 111; tips on government bonds, 87; understanding currencies, 88; vigilance and skepticism of, 64; writing about bonds, 41–45. *See also* reporting business stories; writing business stories
Businessworld (fictional world), xii; banking in, 67; Bankland country profile, 7; Commonland country profile, 4; Energyland country profile, 3; Foodland country profile, 8; map, *xiv–xv*; Netland country profile, 5; Supplyland country profile, 6; for teaching and writing concepts of money, 1–8
buybacks, 49–50
buy side, 117

call options, 126
capital-adequacy requirements, 131
carbon emissions, 63–64
cartograms, 189
cash: financing cash, 63; investments cash, 63; near cash, 61; operations cash, 62. *See also* currencies; money, story of
cash-flow statement, 53, 62–63
catastrophes, 119–20
CDO. *See* collateralized debt obligation
CDS. *See* credit-default swap
central banks, 67, 224; central-bank policies, 12; in Commonland (fictional country), 234; interest rates in, 72, 204; key functions in countries, 71–75; monetary policy of, 71–73
CEO. *See* chief executive officer

charts, 140; bar charts, 186–87, *187*; bubble chart, 189; cartograms, 189; for data presentation, 186–92; dot plot chart, 189; examples, 190–91; heatmaps, 189; histograms, 189; horizontal bar charts, 187, *187*; line charts, 188, *188*, 191; normalized line chart, 188, *188*; pictograms, 189; pie charts, 188–89, *189*; stacked horizontal bar chart, 189; stacked vertical charts, 190; as stand-alone, 186; step chart, 189; tips for creating, 189–90; vertical bar charts, 186, *187*

chief executive officer (CEO), 35, 45, 65; opinions of, 143

clarity, 148

cliches, 163, 177, 200

climate change, xi, 8, 107, 119, 162

Clinton, Bill, 1

CLOs. *See* collateralized loan obligations

collateralized debt obligation (CDO), xi, 112, 130

collateralized loan obligations (CLOs), 130

commercial banks, 116

commodities: crops as, 102–3; demand for products and, 111; extracted commodities, 99; finite resources and, 107–9; grown commodities, 99; hard commodities, 99, *100*; as haven assets, 110; linking to livelihoods, 111; mining and, 104–6; overview, 99; reporting on, 100–102; soft commodities, 99, *100*; strategies around, 111; Your Turn exercises, 104, 106, 109, 110, 227–29

Commonland (fictional country): benchmark interest rate in, 71; central bank, 234; Central Statistics Office in, 70, 77–78, 93; chamber of commerce, 73; *Commonland Express*, 69–70, 73, 76–77, 82–83, 85–86, 91–95, 97, 104, 108, 134, 136–37, 139; country profile, 4; CPI, 203; dollar in, 85; Eatmore Co. example, in, 14, 171, 235; GiantSteel Corp. example, in, 74, 104–5; Inject Inc. example, in, 45, 181, 236; natural resources in, 67; notes in, 87; oil in, 109; payments to families with children, 9; Peak Analytics Co. example, in, 70, 73, 83, 85, 91, 94, 110; Pureoil Co. example, in, 109, 225; Refinery Corp. example, in, 109; reserve bank in, 82–83; Rustic Steel Co. example, in, 77, 104–5; steel in, 104–5; Stellarcars Co. example, in, 74, 77, 90, 134

companies: bond selling by, 35–41, 113; borrowing by, 129; buybacks, 49–50; dividends and, 51–52; earnings and, 53–59; ESG and, 63–65; financial statements and, 60–61; journalist qualities for breaking stories, 34; mergers and acquisitions, 47–48; overview, 34–35; share split and, 47; target company, 47–49; writing about corporate bonds, 41–45; Your Turn exercises, 45, 46, 48, 59, 65, 221–23

comparisons, 64, 177, 183, 190

compelling business stories, 149–51

conjunctions, 199

Consumer Price Index (CPI), 67, 68, 77; calculation of, 80, 82; in Commonland (fictional country), 203; for inflation measurement, 79; in Netland (fictional country), 231

consumers: consumer confidence, 66, 91, 95; consumer price inflation, 80, 82; consumer sentiment, 95; consumer trends, 118

contracts: benchmark contract, 124; forward contract, 125; futures contracts, 99

coronavirus pandemic, xi

corporate activities, 34, 65

corporate bond ratings, 38

corporate paper, 129

costs: non-operating costs, 61; operating costs, 61; spreading costs, 119

countries: budget in, 83–84; central bank functions in, 71–75; consumer confidence in, 95; currencies in, 88–90; fiscal policy in, 83–86; government bonds in, 66, 86–88; housing in, 93; industrial production in, 94; inflation in, 77–83; jobs in, 91–92; legislation in, 96; measurement of economy, 67–70; overview, 66–67; PMI in, 76–77; politics in, 96–98; proxy indicators in, 98; retail sales in, 94; trade in, 92–93; Your Turn exercises, 71, 75, 80–81, 86, 96, 223–26

coupon rate, 37, 42

CPI. *See* Consumer Price Index

credit: creditworthiness, 40; revolving credit lines, 129
credit-default swap (CDS), 127, 129
cryptocurrencies, 121, 131
currencies, 67; business journalists understanding, 88; in countries, 88–90; cryptocurrencies, 121, 131; currency-exchange apps, 121; defined, 88; exchange rates, 89; in Netland (fictional country), 150, 164; reserve currency, *89*; strengthening and weakening of, 90; volatile, 114
current ratio, 62

data presentation: analysis tools, 193; charts and graphics for, 186–92; data sets for, 185–86; marry words with, 193; numeracy skills for, 180–85; overview, 179; Your Turn exercises, 181, 183, 184, 185, 191, 236–37
data sets, 185–86
deadlines, 148
debt, 45; collateralized debt obligation, xi, 112, 130; distressed debt, 130; government, in Netland (fictional country), 221; secured debt, 129; total debt/equity, 62; unsecured debt, 129
deep sourcing, 34
defamation, 14–15
default, 37–38
deflation, 72; GDP deflator, 79
deposits, 116
depreciation, 53, 61–62, 118, 205
derivatives: futures as, 124–25; investments and, 123–27, 132; options as, 126; swaps as, 126–27
differing opinions, 143
digital media, 141–42, 193
diluted earnings per share, 61
discount, 48
distressed debt, 130
dividends: companies and, 51–52; dividend yield, 52; ex-dividend, 52
dot plot chart, 189
Dow Jones Industrial Average, 24

earnings: of banks, 117; companies and, 53–59; diluted earnings per share, 61; earnings season, 63; earnings statement, 58; price/earnings ratio, 29–30, 60; stocks and, 26–27; stories on, 56–59
earnings per share (EPS), 26, 30, 56, 61; calculation of, 182; performance and, 182
economies: economic conditions, 41; economic growth, 66, *166*; economic indicators, 67; economic performance, 89; measurement of, 67–70; politics and, 96–98
editor-in-chief, 194
efficiency ratio, 117, 118
electric car manufacture, 107, 109
Energyland (fictional country): agriculture in, 104; ChemPet Inc. example, in, 168; Commodities Exchange, 102; country profile, 3; dollar in, 85, *89*, 89–90; Gasopolis Asset Management Co. example, in, 67, 95, 109; gold in, 110, 228–29; government in, 153; Keepfit Inc. example, in, 149, 157–58; Mysteak Inc. example, in, 171, 235; natural gas in, 197; oil in, 107–8; protests in, 152, 155; remote areas in, 165; school programs in, 9; Steak N Chips Co. example, in, 171, 235; wheat in, 1–4
enterprise value, 47
environmental social and governance issues (ESG), xi, 63–65
EPS. *See* earnings per share; estimated price/earnings
equities, 17, 19; equity value, 47–48; return on equity, 63; total debt/equity, 62. *See also* shares
ESG. *See* environmental social and governance issues
estimated price/earnings (EPS), 29–30
ETF. *See* exchange-traded fund
excellence, 148, 157
Excel spreadsheets, 185–86
exchange rates, 88, 89
exchange ratio, 48
exchange-traded fund (ETF), 128
ex-dividend, 52
explanatory journalists, x, 177
explanatory podcasts, 146
exports, 92–93
extracted commodities, 99

face value of bonds, 36–38
familiar words, 154

family office, 119
features writer, 194
fees, 118, 120
financial crisis (2008), xi
financial institutions, 70, 112, *115*, 131, 197
financial journalism, ix
financial newsletters, 194
financial regulation, 131–32
financial statements: balance sheet as, 61–62; cash-flow statement, 53; companies and, 60–61; income statement release, 60–61
financial technology (fintech), 121
financing cash, 63
fintech. *See* financial technology
First Amendment, 14
fiscal policy, 67; in countries, 83–86
fiscal year, 53, 83–84
Fitch Ratings, 40
fixed coupon rate of bonds, 38
fixed deposits, 116
fixed interest rate, 126
flash headlines, 159
flexibility, 34
floating interest rate, 126
flow of money, 129
Foodland (fictional country): Brie Inc. example, in, 181; cocoa in, 183, 236; country profile, 8; economic growth, *166*; Fizz Co. example, in, 59, 222–23; Flightco Inc, example, in, 149, 151, 162, 200; Foodie Brokerage Inc., example in, 28–29; *Foodland Times*, 21, 26–29, 31, 35, 37, 46–55, 63–64, 103, 125, 220; Grapeland Valley Winery example, in, 232; misconduct in, 159; national statistics office, 80; Olympics in, 9, 218; Peasplus Corp. example, in, 33, 169, 176, 199, 221, 235; Sip Corp. example, in, 18–20, 23–29, 32, *32*, 34–54, 63–64, 103, 113–14, 126, 165, 184, 220, 229–30, 237; Smart Speakers example in, 225; Snackable Inc. example, in, 24–25, 49–49, 113, 150, 199, 200, 220, 234, 236; stock exchange in, *20*, 24, 28, 33; sugar in, 102–3; Sweeti Inc. example, in, 15, 102–3, 124–25, 174, 201, 234, 235; Toe Stock Broking Co. example, in, 103;

Veggi Co., example, in, 24–25, 28, 47–48, 113, 155, 156; wildfires in, 145, 232
forecast, 26
foreign exchange (forex), 89. *See also* currencies
forward contract, 125
forwards, 124
forward spin, 177
friendly takeover, 48
fundamental analysis of stocks, 31
funds: exchange-traded fund, 128; fund managers, 119; pension fund managers, 119; pension funds, 116, 128–29. *See also* hedge funds; mutual funds
futures, 124–25; futures contracts, 99; futures price, 101

GDP. *See* gross domestic product
GDP deflator, 79
general obligation securities, 130
gold, 110, 228–29
government bonds, 45, 67; auctions for, 87–88, *88*; benchmark bond, 87; in countries, 86–88; tips for business journalists, 87; yields, 87
government policies, 12, 226
graphics, 140
gross domestic product (GDP), 66, 67–69; in Bankland (fictional country), 75; GDP deflator, 77; growth in, 71, 82; as quarterly economic indicator, 76; writing style points for, 70–71
grown commodities, 99

hacks, 138–39
hard commodities, 99, *100*
haven assets, 110
headlines: avoiding clutter in, 161–62; avoiding puns, jargon, alliteration, 163; avoiding unfamiliar acronyms, 162; avoiding unfamiliar names, 163; in business stories, 158–65; for digital media, 141; flash headlines, 159; geared to audience, 159–61, 164; leads consistent with, 170; limit labels in, 163; rule of thumb for, 159–60; surprise in, 164; understandable theme, 160–61; what plus formula for, *160*

heatmaps, 189
hedge funds: business journalists reporting on, 120, 132; investments and, *115*, 116, 120; performance of, 120
hedging, 110
high-yield bonds, 41. *See also* junk bonds
histograms, 189
hoaxes, 138–39
horizontal bar charts, 187, *187*
hostile takeover, 48
house prices, 66; in Bankland (fictional country), 236
housing starts, 93
hype, 200–201
hyphenated words, 202

imports, 92
income, 56; net interest income, 117. *See also* net income
income statement, 53; cash-flow statement as, 62–63; release, 60–61
industrial production, 94
inflation, 7, 66, 67; consumer price inflation, 80, 82; in countries, 77–83; CPI for measuring, 79; interest rates and, 74; stoking of, 72. *See also* deflation
inflows, 128
initial public offering (IPO), 17, 122; defined, 19; early steps of, *20*; first sales, 18–20; pricing of, 20–22; reporting on, 21–22; stock exchange and, 23–24
insider trading, 131
institutional investors, 22, 116
insurers, *115*, 116, 119–20
intangible assets, 62
interest rates: benchmark interest rates, 71, 72, 74; in central banks, 72, 204; fixed interest rate, 126; floating interest rate, 126; inflation and, 74; interest-rate swap, 126; repo rate, 73
international trading, 7
internet banks, 121
interns, 193
interviews: beginning for, 134; for business stories, 134–36; as conversation, 134; preparation, 134; questions for, 135–36
inventories, 62
investments: borrowing and, 129–31; derivatives and, 123–27, 132; exchange-traded fund, 128; financial institutions for, *115*; financial regulation of, 131–32; hedge funds and, *115*, 116, 120; institutional investors, 116; insurers and, 119–20; investment banks, 115–17; investment grades, 40; investments cash, 63; investor relations, ix; money managers and, 119; Moody's Investors Service, 40; mutual funds and, 120, 127–28; non-investment grades, 40; overview, 112–14; pension funds as, 116, 128–29; private equity firms and, 121; strategies for, 119; venture capital and, 122; Your Turn exercises, 114, 118, 122, 126, 132, 229–30
IPO. *See* initial public offering
issue price, 38

jargon: avoiding, in headlines, 142, 163; in business stories, 201
jobs, 66; in countries, 91–92; joblessness, 5, 91–92
journalese, 200
junk bonds, 40–41
Junnarkar, Sandeep, 185

key performance indicators (KPIs), 29, 35, 60, 68
keywords, 141
kicker quote, 175–76
KPIs. *See* key performance indicators

lagging economic indicator, 67
language prompts, 173
LBO. *See* leveraged-buyout
leading indicator, 77
lead manager, 19, *20*, 23
leads: active verbs for, 154–55; active voice for, 155–56; attribution in, 168; avoiding word echoes in, 152; big picture idea in, 152; in business stories, 150–58, 165–70; clear theme in, 167; consistent with headlines, 170; familiar words for, 154; momentum of, 169–70; precision in, 157–58; rewriting subordinate clauses, 152; rhythm for, 169; sense of direction in, 167; short sentences for, 151–54; solving problems with,

151–58; superlatives for, 156–57, 164; surprise in, 165, 167; thinking like editor for, *166*; tone set in, 165; unexpected in, 169; what, why, so-what in, 168; in writing business stories, 150–58
legislation, in countries, 96
length: in reporting business stories, 144; in writing business stories, 176
leveraged-buyout (LBO), 121
libel, 15
line charts, 188, *188*, 191
liquidity ratio, 62
long-term borrowings, 62

M&A. *See* merger and acquisition
market-moving news, 98, 143, 159
market speculation, 28–29
mean, 184–85
median, 68, 184–85
merger and acquisition (M&A), 132
mergers, 47–48
mining, 104–6
mobile payment networks, 121
mode, 184–85
MoM. *See* month-on-month
momentum: of leads, 169–70; in second paragraph of business story, 171
monetary policies, 67; of central banks, 71–73. *See also* fiscal policy
money, story of: best practices in, 13–15; business angles in every story, 10; Businessworld for teaching and writing concepts, 1–8; finding stories, 12; flow of money, 129; follow the money, 1, 23, 96, 193; making connections in, 9; numbers in, 11–12; pool money, 121; so what in every story, 11; Your Turn exercises, 9, 13, 15, 217–19
money laundering, 131, 162
money managers, *115*, 119
money markets, 129
month-on-month (MoM), 203
Moody's Investors Service, 40
multimedia, ix, 177
municipal bonds, 130
mutual funds, 120, 128; performance of, 127

names: in business stories, 200; unfamiliar, in headlines, 163
natural resources, 4

NAV. *See* net asset value
near cash, 61
net asset value (NAV), 127
net fixed assets, 61–62
net income, 26; net income attributable to common shareholders, adjusted, 53; net income growth, 60–61
net interest income, 117
Netland (fictional country): country profile, 5; CPI, 231; currency, 150, 164; dollar in, 161; Driverless Inc. example, in, 48, 155; electric car manufacture, 107, 109; GDP in, 159; government bonds in, 45; government debt, 221; illicit finance in, 131–32; Imps Inc. example, in, 152, 184, 237; profits in, 142; rent increases in, 9; retail crisis in, 154; Robo Corp. example, in, 80, 134, 157, 169, 234; Shirtz Co. example, in, 154; Squeaker example in, 10, *10*, 103, 226, 231; Web Co. example, in, 48; Websville example in, 152–53
news judgment, 34, 194
non-investment grades, 40
non-news words, 197
non-operating costs, 61
normalized line chart, 188, *188*
notes, 62
numeracy skills: EPS calculation, 182; mean, median, mode differences, 184–85; numbers coming alive, 183–84; number usage, 182–83; percentage change calculation, 180–82
nut paragraph, *See* big-picture paragraph

offer, 23–24
offering memorandum, 37
oil, 107–9
open market operations, 71, 72
operations: operating costs, 61; operating margin, 61; operations cash, 62
options, 126
outflows, 128
overused words, phrases, 196–97
Oxford English Dictionary, 145

paragraphs: second paragraph, in business story, 171–72; to-be-sure paragraph, 177. *See also* big-picture paragraph

par value, 37
P/E. *See* price/earnings ratio
pension fund managers, 119
pension funds, 116, 128–29
percentage change calculation, 180–82
performance: of banks, 117; of bonds, 41, 42, *42*; economic performance, 89; EPS and, 182; of hedge funds, 120; key performance indicators, 29, 35, 60, 68; of mutual funds, 127; of stocks, 27
pictograms, 189
pie charts, 188–89, *189*
PMI. *See* Purchasing Managers Index
podcasts, ix, 133, 134, 210, 211, 213, 214; adding to story, 150, 177; explanatory, 146; producers, x, 194; roundtable, 146; target audience for, 145; tone and format for, 146
politics: in action, 97–98; all politics is local, 97; in countries, 96–98; economies and, 67, 96–98
pool money, 121
precision in leads, 157–58
preliminary prospectus, 20, *20*
premiums, 48, 119
prepositions, 199
price/earnings ratio (P/E), 29–30, 60
prices: benchmark price, 101; bond prices, 41, 42; consumer price inflation, 80, 82; estimated price/earnings, 29–30; futures price, 101; home prices, 236; house prices, 66; issue price, 38; price band, 21; price changes, 101; share-price reaction, 57; spot price, 101; word usage, 141. *See also* Consumer Price Index
privacy, 14–15
private brokers, 116
private equity, 121; private equity firms, *115*
private placement of bonds, 36
private pools of capital, 120
profit: expressions of, 56; in Netland (fictional country), 142; profit margins, 12, 61; words, in business stories, 204–5
proprietary trading, 116
prospectus, 37
protection, for story sources, 137
protectionism, 92

proxy indicators, 98
public interest, 15
public issue of bonds, 36–37
public relations, ix, 113, 133, 138, 175, 235
puns, 142, 163
Purchasing Managers Index (PMI), 66, 76–77
put options, 126

QoQ. *See* quarter-on-quarter
quantitative easing, xi
quantitative literacy, 179
quarter-on-quarter (QoQ), 67, 203
quotations: in business stories, 174–76; keys to using in stories, 175; kicker quote, 175–76; never repeat, change, or add to, 174

radio reporting, 145
real GDP, 67–69
red herring, 20, *20*
regulations, 119; financial regulation, 131–32; legislation, in countries, 96. *See also* fiscal policy; monetary policies
regulator, *20*, 20–21
relative pronouns, 199–200
relative strength index (RSI), 31–32, *32*
renewable energy, 108
repo rate, 73
reporting business stories: anonymous sources in, 136–38; attribution for, 144; on banks, 117–18; brainstorming in, 147; on commodities, 100–102; cross-platforms for, 139–40; digital media in, 141–42; on hedge funds, 120, 132; hoaxes and hacks in, 138–39; interviews for, 23, 27, 134–36; on IPOs, 21–22; key role of, 147; on legislation, 96; length of story, 144; overview, 133–34; podcasts for, 145–46; practical tips for, 141–42; print for, 140; radio, 145; social media and, 138–39; structure in, 144; style for television and radio, 144; on supply and demand, 111; television, 143–44; tense in, 144; Your Turn exercises, 136, 139, 142, 146, 230–33
reserve currency, *89*
reserve requirements, 71
resource conservation, 64
retail sales, 66, 94

return on equity, 63
revenue passenger miles (RPM), 60
revenues: average revenue per unit/user, 60; defined, 53; revenue growth, 60; trading revenue, 117. *See also* sales
revolving credit lines, 129
roundtable podcasts, 146
RPM. *See* revenue passenger miles
RSI. *See* relative strength index

safe haven, 110
sales: bond 88, 299; defined, 53; forecast/target, 44–45, 77, 113; in American English vs. British English, 195; retail 68, 94; slowdown in, 74; and trade, 92; writing about, 54–55, 154, 157–58; *See also* revenue
scams, 131
search engine optimization (SEO), 141
seasonally adjusted data, 67–68
second paragraph in business story, 171–72
secured debt, 129
securities, 17; asset-backed security, 129; general obligation securities, 130
sell side, 117
senior reporter, 194
sense of direction, 167
SEO. *See* search engine optimization
shared risk, 130
shares, 17, 19; diluted earnings per share, 61; share-price reaction, 57; shares outstanding, 22; share split, 47; value, 46; why shares move, 25–26. *See also* earnings per share
short-selling, 120
show, don't tell, 15
skepticism, 34
slander, 15
social media, 138–39
soft commodities, 99, *100*
sources: anonymous, 136–38; best practices for, 13; building, 65, 132; protection of, 137
sovereign bond, 38
S&P 500 Index, 24
S&P Global Ratings, 40
spot price, 101
spread: bonds, yield and, 43–45; defined, 44; spreading costs, 119
stacked horizontal bar chart, 189
stacked vertical charts, 190
step chart, 189

stock exchange: in Foodland (fictional country), *20*, 24, 28, 33; IPO and, 23–24
stocks: earnings and, 26–27; explain broader significance when reporting, 25; follow money when reporting, 23; historic performance of, 27; IPO offering, 18–20; IPO pricing, 20–22; market speculation and, 28–29; overview, 17; rise and fall of, 25; risks with, 86; start of company, 17–18; stock index and, 24–25, 27; stock market, 24, 33; technical analysis of, 31–33; valuation and, 29–30; why in reporting on, 27; why shares move, 25–26; Your Turn exercises, 24, 25, 33, 220–21. *See also* bonds; shares
storytellers, 167
structure: in reporting business stories, 144; structured finance, 130
style: for commonly used terms, 202–3; for television and radio, 144; writing about GDP, 70–71
subordinate clauses, 152
superlatives, 156–57, 164
supply and demand, 12, 23–24
Supplyland (fictional country): Chip Co. example, in, 168; country profile, 6; deep bond market in, 36; forecasts for, 185; Linen Co. example, in, 170, 235; Phonz Inc. example, in, *42*, 42–43, 80; trade deficit in, 183; Wear Inc. example, in, 10–12, 46, 184, 222; women's wages in, 9
surprise: in headlines, 164; in leads, 165, 167
swaps, 124, 126–27
syndicate, 19, *20*
syndicated loan, 129

takeovers, 48
target company, 47–49, 121
teaching guide: for one-day training courses, 213; for one-week training courses, 213–14; for ten weeks, 214–15. *See also* Your Turn exercises
technical analysis of stocks, 31–33
technology: blockchain technology, 121; financial technology, 121;
television reporting, 143–44
tense, in business stories, 144
term loans, 129

time, writing of, 205
titles, 205
to-be-sure paragraph, 177
total debt/equity, 62
total return, 51
trade, 66; in countries, 92–93; deficit, in Supplyland (fictional country), 183; exchange-traded fund, 128; insider trading, 131; international trading, 7; proprietary trading, 116; trade publications, 194; trade wars, 92; trading revenue, 117
transparency: of attribution, 137; ESG transparency, 64; transparency with sources, 13
transaction value, 47

underwriter, 19–20; underwriting bonds, 36
unemployment, 66, 91
unsecured debt, 129

vague words, 198
valuation, 29–30
value: enterprise value, 47; equity value, 47–48; face value of bonds, 36–38; par value, 37; of shares, 46; transaction value, 47
venture capital (VC), 122
verbs, 198
vertical bar charts, 186, *187*
visual images, 140, 143. *See also* data presentation
volunteerism, 64

wealth managers, 119
what plus formula, *160*
whistleblowers, 65
word echoes, 152
words in business stories: American English compared to British English, 195; cliches, 200; conjunctions and prepositions, 199; hype, 200–201; hyphenated words, 202; jargon, 201; journalese, 200; names, 200; non-news words, 197; numbers, 203–4; overused words and phrases, 196–97;

percent and percentage points, 204; profit, 204–5; relative pronouns, 199–200; rounding numbers, 204; style for commonly used terms, 202–3; time, 205; titles, 205; vague words, 198; verbs to watch, 198
workplace discrimination, 64
writing business stories: A+B+C+D+E formula for, 148; anecdotes in, 177; big-picture paragraph, 172–74; bullet points in, 177; comparisons in, 177; compelling stories, 149–51; forward spin in, 177; good writing for, 177–78; headlines in, 150, 158–65; leads in, 150–58, 165–70; length of story, 176; multimedia for, 177; one thought per sentence in, 151; overview, 148; quotations in, 174–76; secondary big-picture paragraph for, 176; second paragraph in, 171–74; simple, short, sharp stories, 149–51; to-be-sure paragraph in, 177; Your Turn exercises, 150, 156, 157, 161, 165, 170, 171, 176, 234–35. *See also* best practices in story writing; words in business stories

year-on-year (YoY), 68, 71, 203
yield: bonds and, 38–39, *39*; dividend yield, 52; for government bonds, 87; high-yield bonds, 41; spread and, 43–45; yield to maturity, 41
Your Turn exercises: answer key, 217–37; for commodities, 104, 106, 109, 110, 227–29; for companies, 45, 46, 48, 59, 65, 221–23; for countries, 71, 75, 80–81, 86, 96, 223–26; for data presentation, 181, 183, 184, 185, 191, 236–37; for investments, 114, 118, 122, 126, 132, 229–30; for reporting business stories, 136, 139, 142, 146, 230–33; for stocks, 24, 25, 33, 220–21; for story of money, 9, 13, 15, 217–19; for writing business stories, 150, 156, 157, 161, 165, 170, 171, 176, 234–35
YoY. *See* year-on-year

GPSR Authorized Representative: Easy Access System Europe, Mustamäe tee
50, 10621 Tallinn, Estonia, gpsr.requests@easproject.com

www.ingramcontent.com/pod-product-compliance
Lightning Source LLC
Chambersburg PA
CBHW022046290426
44109CB00014B/999